8 Mighty Changes
God Wants for You

Before
You Get to
Heaven

D. KELLY OGDEN

DESERET
BOOK

SALT LAKE CITY, UTAH

Excerpt from "A Masque of Reason," from *The Poetry of Robert Frost,* edited by
Edward Connery Lathem. Copyright 1945 by Robert Frost, copyright 1969 by
Henry Holt and Company, copyright 1973 by Lesley Frost Ballantine. Reprinted
by permission of Henry Holt and Company, LLC.

Library of Congress Cataloging-in-Publication Data

Ogden, D. Kelly (Daniel Kelly), 1947–
  Before you get to heaven : 8 mighty changes God wants for you / D. Kelly
Ogden.
      p. cm.
  Includes bibliographical references and index.
  ISBN-10 1-59038-337-0 (hardcover : alk. paper)
  ISBN-13 978-1-59038-337-7 (hardcover : alk. paper)
  1. Christian life—Biblical teaching. I. Title.
  BS680.C47O37 2004
  248.4'89332—dc22
                                        2004008447

Printed in the United States of America
Publishers Printing, Salt Lake City, UT

10   9   8   7   6   5

CONTENTS

Contents

INTRODUCTION

AFTER LIVING AND WORKING IN THE Holy Land for most of fourteen years, I returned with my family to Provo, Utah, and I was called to serve in a branch presidency at the Missionary Training Center. That means that after living nearly a decade and a half in a land where *no* missionary work is done, I would be serving in a place where *only* missionary work is done!

I thought I would go in there and teach those elders and sisters a thing or two they had never heard before, tantalizing them with some intellectual morsels they could write home about. However, it took me a very short time to realize that what they really needed wasn't the historical and political background of Isaiah's messianic prophecies to King Ahab, or a treatise on light, fire, and cloud phenomena at the appearance and disappearance of celestial beings, or the symbolic language and figures of speech used in Jesus' parables (as fascinating as all those things are); what they needed was an understanding of how to really repent, how to obtain and keep the Spirit, how to get rid of pride, how to really pray, how to be strictly obedient, and how to not just "get along" with but truly learn to love a companion and other people.

As I taught my scripture courses at Brigham Young University over the following years, I realized that that is what those students also needed, more than anything else. Serving with more than five hundred elders and sisters for three years in the nation of Chile reinforced that conclusion many times over. At last, I've become convinced that those are the same messages all of us Saints need to learn and live.

That's the rationale behind this book. Right here and now, before we get to heaven, we all need to learn how to achieve mighty scripture study and mighty prayer, to exercise mighty faith and mighty repentance. We all must learn how to obtain and keep the Spirit, how to be exactly obedient, how to get rid of pride, and how to get the love of God in us.

Studying and desiring to live all these things will produce mighty changes in us, which changes will likewise influence the lives of many others of Heavenly Father's children. The Father and the Savior have provided the necessary instruction and have shown us the way; now it's our choice—to learn it, love it, and live it.

1

HOW TO HAVE MIGHTY SCRIPTURE STUDY

IF ELDER BRUCE R. MCCONKIE WERE ASKED, "How do you know so much about the scriptures?" he would answer, "I read them."[1] The fact is (as we reluctantly point out), the Latter-day Saints generally know the gospel is true, but they don't know the gospel. Certainly our spiritual witness, our testimony, is most important, but even better is to have a knowledge-solid testimony. The more gospel knowledge you have, the stronger your spiritual witness can be. Pardon the expression, but in the Church it really would be wonderful to have more than "punch and cookie" testimonies. True spirituality is not born out of ignorance. We would all be better Latter-day Saints if we knew the scriptures better.

On September 5, 1999, we held a conference of all the

sister missionaries in the Chile Santiago East Mission, over which we presided. Sister Ogden was conducting the conference and wrote the following about an experience she had in connection with the conference:

"I hadn't planned on speaking in this conference but when I woke up at 4:30 this morning the thoughts really started coming and I started writing.

"I had just studied Doctrine and Covenants 24 and 25 the day before. If you ask people to name what section 25 is about they will immediately respond, 'Hymns.' I came across something a hundred times meatier than hymns in verses 7 and 8. The Lord is telling Emma that she is set apart to expound the scriptures and to exhort the Church according as it is given her by the Spirit. She is to give her time to much writing and much learning. Wow. Think about it—this is the 1800s, when no one expected a woman to preach and teach.

"I told the sisters that Doctrine and Covenants 25 is a call to every woman to really study the scriptures and make a contribution wherever she resides, that if they would make scripture study a life-long habit they would become wells of living water springing up unto everlasting life—not only for themselves, but for all who would come into their association.

People would drink deeply from their depths and they would be a life-giving influence wherever they served.

"Reading the scriptures every day—I mean studying, not nibbling—seems to make you 'ready always to give an answer to every man that asketh you a reason of the hope that is in you' (1 Peter 3:15). It worked for me early this morning. The thoughts and scriptures that came to mind had long been planted there by many scripture study sessions. God can't help us reap what hasn't been sown."

WHY SHOULD WE STUDY THE SCRIPTURES?

I have written in the front of my Bible and in the front of my triple combination five reasons we should study the scriptures:

1. *"Search the scriptures" is a commandment* (see John 5:39), not a suggestion. Way back in an early dispensation the Lord counseled: "This book of the law shall not depart out of thy mouth; but thou shalt meditate therein day and night, that thou mayest observe to do according to all that is written therein: for then thou shalt make thy way prosperous, and then thou shalt have good success" (Joshua 1:8).

2. *We will be judged from these books.* "For behold, out of

the books which have been written, and which shall be written, shall this people be judged" (3 Nephi 27:25). There are millions of books printed with the words of men; there are four books with the words of God. If we really believe that we will be judged from what is written in those four books, we will want to know what is in them.

3. *If we don't study these things, we are showing a lack of love for God.* Why? Because he spent thousands of years preparing and preserving and transmitting these sacred writings to us in the last days. The Old Testament record—Moses to Malachi—was in preparation for more or less a thousand years. The Book of Mormon record—Lehi to Moroni—was also a thousand years. That's a lot of time, of some of the best people's lives, to get the Lord's words to us, and if we don't even pick them up and find out what is in them, we are definitely showing a lack of love for and appreciation to God.

4. *By reading the scriptures we can testify that we have heard the voice of Christ.* That's what Doctrine and Covenants 18:34–36 says. The words of scripture are the voice of Christ to us, and his voice can speak to us personally.

5. *Answers to many of our questions and problems are in the scriptures.* Nephi wrote, "Feast upon the words of Christ; for

behold, the words of Christ will tell you all things what ye should do" (2 Nephi 32:3). And if you can't seem to find a specific answer to some dilemma, while studying the Savior's words you are entitled to have the Spirit of the Lord come over you, and he "will show unto you all things what ye should do" (2 Nephi 32:5).

Elder Boyd K. Packer said: "For His own reasons, the Lord provides answers to some questions, with pieces placed here and there throughout the scriptures. We are to find them; we are to *earn* them. In that way sacred things are hidden from the insincere."[2]

Elder Bruce R. McConkie warned that even those immersed in Church leadership have to spend the necessary effort to search the scriptures: "May I suggest, based on personal experience, that faith comes and revelations are received as a direct result of scriptural study. . . . However talented men may be in administrative matters; however eloquent they may be in expressing their views; however learned they may be in worldly things—they will be denied the sweet whisperings of the Spirit that might have been theirs unless they pay the price of studying, pondering, and praying about the scriptures."[3]

How to Make Your Scripture Study "Mighty"

1. *Use more of your five physical senses.* Psychologists tell us that the more of our five physical senses we use, the more we learn. Those senses include sight, hearing, smelling, tasting, and touching. You learn more through your eyes than any other part of your body, but if you can use other senses you will increase your ability to absorb intellectual and spiritual treasures. For example, take the sense of hearing. God blessed us with two ears as well as two eyes. Besides reading with your eyes, if you will read aloud you will learn more. Before I married, a friend and I read the entire Old Testament aloud. It took several months; in fact, it does take longer reading that way, but by involving one more of your physical senses you will find yourself "seeing" more in the scriptures than ever before.

You can also use your sense of touch by having a red pencil or a fine-point pen in hand as you read the scriptures. Underline, color in, cross-reference, or take notes in your margins. Keep your hands busy as well as your eyes, and you will learn more.

2. *Write your impressions—the revelation that comes while*

reading. While you are studying the scriptures, you are entitled to receive the Spirit; and while you are feeling the Spirit, revelation will come. We are all writing our own "book of revelation." Keep a notebook, any kind of notebook, right alongside your scriptures, and during your reading, stop and ponder what you read. As impressions come to you, write them down. They may be thoughts about what you are reading. Or, while you are "in the Spirit," the Lord may reveal something to you that actually has nothing to do with what is written on the page you are studying—but it will generally have something to do with your life, something specific the Lord wants to tell you. Sometimes we may think as impressions come, "Don't distract me, Lord, I'm studying the scriptures!"—and he can't get through to us. Don't get too busy going through the motions that you cannot receive revelation when he wants to send it. Joseph Smith once warned, "For neglecting to write these things when God had revealed them, not esteeming them of sufficient worth, the Spirit may withdraw and God may be angry."[4]

A missionary wrote to me: "President, for more than half a year now I've had a question I couldn't answer. But during your talk to our stake youth, the Lord gave me the answer. It wasn't anything grand; actually it was something quite simple.

And it all happened because I was *writing* what came to my mind, as you told us to do. I have so much enthusiasm and personal revelation about what I can do—now that I'm writing down what the Lord tells me."

Remember: your scripture study time is not a race. I used to mark all those little charts and squares and color-in schemes for each chapter, to keep me on schedule and meeting my quota and reading the four standard works once a year or some other such regimen. I've changed my mind. I don't try to adhere to any strict quantity in scripture reading any more, because I want to stop and ponder and write about what I am thinking and feeling. A strict one-page-a-day or one-chapter-a-day schedule may inhibit your taking the time to ponder, as well as inhibiting the free flow of revelation.

3. *Pray, meditate, write about the scriptures, and teach your impressions to others.* Pray for guidance in your study of the Lord's words. I know one leader in the Church who prays over each page; as he turns each page he offers a little prayer that he will gain something wonderful from that page. After you have prayed and paused to reflect on what you are learning, and after you have written some of your new understanding, make a point of teaching the new idea or revelation that has come to you to another person—your spouse,

roommate, family member, friend, anyone. By teaching a principle to someone else, it will cement the concept even more in your own mind. (Caution: Sometimes the Lord will reveal something to you that he does not want you to share with others. Be discerning and careful about what to share from personal revelation.)

THE LORD'S PROMISES FOR MIGHTY SCRIPTURE STUDY

As you pray, ponder the scriptures, and pen your thoughts, the Lord will show you great things—maybe simple things, but also profound. Consider the following testimonials from some of our scriptural heroes of the past.

Nephi explained: "After I had *desired* to know the things that my father had seen, and *believing* that the Lord was able to make them known unto me, as I sat *pondering* in mine heart I was caught away in the Spirit of the Lord, yea, into an exceedingly high mountain" (1 Nephi 11:1; emphasis added). Then follows the grand panoramic vision the Lord gave to Nephi, chapter after chapter of what we call history, but what he might call "prophetic preview." All this was opened up to him because he desired it, was believing, and took time to ponder on the things of the Lord.

On February 16, 1832, Joseph Smith and Sidney Rigdon were working on the Prophet's inspired revision of the biblical text, specifically the Gospel of John. As they came to a particular verse (John 5:29), they stopped to ponder the meaning of the Lord's teaching. "And while we meditated upon these things, the Lord touched the eyes of our understandings and they were opened, and the glory of the Lord shone round about" (D&C 76:19). Then opened up to them the grand vision of the degrees of glory, one of the greatest of all the revelations that have come in our day. All this happened because they desired it, were believing, and paused to meditate upon the words of scripture.

There have been several Joseph Smiths in our dispensation. One of them, President Joseph F. Smith, was sitting in his home in Salt Lake City, on October 3, 1918, pondering the scriptures. He was particularly reflecting on the words of Peter about Christ's visit to the spirit world between his death and resurrection (see 1 Peter 3:18–20; 4:6). "As I pondered over these things which are written, the eyes of my understanding were opened, and the Spirit of the Lord rested upon me, and I saw the hosts of the dead" (D&C 138:11)—and he described in greater detail than anyone has in all of scripture how the Lord's work is being done in the world of spirits and who is doing it. He specifically noted how the Savior organized the hosts of the righteous to carry on the teaching of the gospel and how the dead were prepared to receive their saving ordinances. All of that was opened to him because he desired it, was believing, and paid the price to stop and ponder the teachings of the scriptures.

One more example: As a boy, Joseph Smith enjoyed studying the Bible. One day he was reading the letter of James, where the ancient church leader encouraged anyone who lacked wisdom to ask of God, and God would respond (see James 1:5). Young Joseph wrote what happened inside him after he read those words: "Never did any passage of scripture come with more power to the heart of man than this did at this time to mine. It seemed to enter with great force into every feeling of my heart. I reflected on it again and again" (Joseph Smith—History 1:12). Notice that the Prophet's history doesn't say that he read that powerful verse, closed his Bible, and dashed into the grove of trees and immediately knelt to pray. It was some time later that he went to pray, because he said that he "reflected on it again and again"—the words just kept working their way into his consciousness; he couldn't get them out of his mind. The Spirit of the Lord carried those words deep into young Joseph's heart and caused him to act on them. The eventual result was the great visitation in the Sacred Grove, followed by many other visitors and revelations from the heavenly world, along with conferral of power (the priesthood), translation and publication of more of the Savior's words, and the beginning of the restoration of all things. All of that happened because of the boy's initial desire, his believing heart, and his ponderings over a single verse of scripture.

The Lord will indeed show unto us great things as we do our part: praying over and studying and reflecting upon the words of scripture—and taking the time to be "in the Spirit."

Jesus Christ has given us a remarkable promise: "Whoso treasureth up my word, shall not be deceived" (Joseph Smith—Matthew 1:37). With all the deceit in the world, that is a comforting assurance, a veritable guarantee: anyone who treasures up (notice he didn't say just "reads" or "studies," but one who *treasures up*) the Savior's words will not be deceived. We need not worry about those who love the scriptures and spend time to study and ponder them. Things will go well for them spiritually. That doesn't mean they will have no problems. We are here in mortality to encounter and learn to deal with problems, challenges, ordeals, even painful afflictions. But in the end (as well as along the way), it will be well for those who love the Lord enough to dedicate the necessary effort to treasuring up his words.

We all know of the tragedy that occurred in the life of King David—which happened in part because he slipped in his study of the scriptures. In his early life he was very close to the Lord. Based on the historical record and his own writings (for example, many psalms), we know he developed a deep and abiding relationship with God and had received numerous revelations. The Spirit guided his life for years. But somehow that relationship deteriorated. I know two things that happened: he stopped praying, and he stopped studying the scriptures. It doesn't say that in the biblical text, but I can read between the lines, and I know perfectly well that David had stopped those two essential habits—prayer and scripture study—and the tragedy ensued. If he had been praying sincerely every day, if he had been treasuring up the Lord's words every day, the ugly events that followed would likely not have happened. The king could have had the spiritual strength to resist the great temptation when it came.

The Lord revealed to Nephi that "whoso would hearken unto the word of God, and would hold fast to it, they would never perish; neither could the temptations and the fiery darts of the adversary overpower them unto blindness, to lead them away to destruction" (1 Nephi 15:24). How's that for a promise! Hold fast to the word of God and you *cannot perish.* Hold tight to the word of God and Satan's fiery darts *cannot overpower you.* And what are those "fiery darts" today? Immoral and violent movies, pornographic Internet sites, worldly music, and crude language—to name a few. They are numerous, widespread, and vicious. But they cannot harm you if you avoid them, which you will do if you are staying close to the Lord—and his words in four books of scripture will keep you close to him.

Personal Examples of Pondering the Scriptures

One morning during my personal scripture study I didn't get past the first verse I read, which was Matthew 8:1: "When he was come down from the mountain, great multitudes followed him." I pondered; then I wrote: "We must climb to the mountain top (for example, the temple), where the Lord will show unto us great things. As Nephi exclaimed, 'I, Nephi, did go into the mount oft, and I did pray oft unto the Lord; wherefore the Lord showed unto me great things' (1 Nephi 18:3). Then we must go back down among the people. There, because we will be full of the Spirit, great multitudes will desire to follow us into the kingdom. We must desire with all our heart to go to the mountain top, then go back down and lead others up."

Another day I was reflecting on Isaiah 48:10, which says, "Behold, I have refined thee, but not with silver; I have chosen thee in the furnace of affliction." Refineries heat metal to its melting point, at which time the impurities separate. Just as gold or silver is smelted in the fire to remove impurities, so God's people are tried with fire to remove impurities. Those impurities (weaknesses, faults) get burned away *if* we can withstand the heat and pressure of our trials. God therefore "turns up the heat" until we reach the point where we become refined so we can be of use to him. The temperature necessary to refine us is different for each person. Our *refinement* is customized for each of us by a perfect and omniscient Father.

To use a different metaphor, just as a diamond is carefully faceted and polished to reveal its inner beauty, so has Israel been shaped and polished. Trials are not punishments inflicted by a vengeful God, but tests by a loving Father who wants us to be refined and polished. Isaiah's words help us know that troubles and trials are purposeful; we endure them for good reasons.

COUNSEL FROM OUR LEADERS

To conclude this chapter, let's consider two testimonies from latter-day prophets, both of which underscore the great need for mighty scripture study in our lives. The first is from Elder Boyd K. Packer, who taught a concept that has become well known in the Church and is a superb example of the revelation that comes through our prophets: "The study of the doctrines of the gospel will improve behavior quicker than a study of behavior will improve behavior. . . . That is why we stress so forcefully the study of the doctrines of the gospel."[5]

And President Harold B. Lee admonished us to include the Lord's words in all we do: "All that we teach in this Church ought to be couched in the scriptures. . . . If we want to measure truth, we should measure it by the four standard works."[6]

2

HOW TO HAVE MIGHTY PRAYER

THESE ARE DANGEROUS TIMES IN which we live. When my daughter Sara was only four years old, we accompanied the Jerusalem Branch Boy Scouts on an overnight campout and fishing trip to the northeastern corner of the Sea of Galilee, near the site of ancient Bethsaida and near where the Jordan River enters the lake. While the boys were out fishing one day, pulling in some big catfish, maybe a St. Peter's fish or two, Sara and I went for a walk. I wanted to walk less than a quarter of a mile west from our camp and try to find the mouth of the Jordan River, where it flows into the lake. Our way was blocked by thickets of tall canes or reeds, and after some time fighting our way through the thick jungle of reeds and tangling undergrowth, knowing we must be very close to the river, we found that it was simply impossible to move forward. We were stuck in the middle of the tall thickets, unable to see in any direction and hardly able to move. I was tired, totally out of energy, and perplexed. Sara looked up at me and said: "Daddy, why don't we pray?"

We folded our arms and prayed, asking Heavenly Father to help us find our way safely out of the thick tangle of vegetation. We forged on, back in the general direction toward our camp, until we came to a barbed-wire fence. Having maneuvered our way over the fence, I looked back and noticed on the fence the internationally recognized triangular-shaped sign for a minefield. *We had just made our way through a minefield.* Needless to say, I was thankful for a daughter who had suggested we pray, and for a Father who had answered our prayer.

The scriptures say this world is a field (see Matthew 13:38; D&C 86:2); and these days it is a minefield! How do you avoid stepping in the wrong places? Be sure you are staying morally clean. Be sure you are studying the scriptures, fasting, keeping the Sabbath day holy, serving others, and (if you are endowed) worshipping in the temple. And be sure you go each day to the "throne of grace" (Hebrews 4:16) and send up your petitions to the Lord. If you are not trying to do all these things, you can be sure that you will be stepping into dangerous situations. If you are trying to do all these things, then you are "worthy to stand."

What the Lord Says about Prayer

Have you ever studied one particular topic all through the scriptures? It is a real eye-opener to see the big picture of what the Lord says when you look at one subject at a time. Some time ago I looked up every passage I could find about prayer, and then I organized the results into a study on prayer that I have given to many hundreds of students. I believe prayer is one of the most important subjects we can research in the scriptures. (A copy of that study, titled "What the Lord Says about Prayer," is included among the appendices at the end of this book.)

Following are some specific insights I gained from reviewing all those passages about prayer:

By praying we can gain a testimony through the Spirit (see Alma 5:43–47).

We can pray to avoid temptation and being taken captive by the devil (see 3 Nephi 18:15, 18–19).

We should pray to be filled with the love of Christ; and

we can keep that love inside us by constant attention to prayer (see Moroni 7:48; 8:26).

We can study a matter out in our minds and then ask if it is right; in response, the Lord will give us a feeling (see D&C 9:7–9).

We should avoid being hypocritical or showy, and we should avoid using vain repetitions. We need to get past cliché-level prayer (see Matthew 6:5–8).

We should pray with a believing attitude (see Mark 11:24).

If we want to know something and ask of God with faith, he will give it to us (see James 1:5–8).

We should ask God with faith and with diligence in keeping the commandments (see 1 Nephi 15:7–11).

We should call on God daily with faith and with humility (see Mosiah 4:11).

We should acknowledge our unworthiness before God (see Alma 38:13–14).

In prayer, we should avoid "multiplying words," and we should let the Spirit guide our prayers (see 3 Nephi 19:24–25, 32–33). Feelings are more important than words.

It doesn't do any good just to go through the motions;

prayers don't count unless we really mean what we say (see Moroni 7:6–9).

We are commanded to pray for those who despitefully use us and persecute us (see 3 Nephi 12:44).

We can pray to know the truth of the Book of Mormon (see Moroni 10:4).

We can pray for forgiveness of sins and to know our standing before God (see Joseph Smith—History 1:29).

If we pray, the Lord can show us great things (see 1 Nephi 18:3).

We can have great understandings revealed to us; prayer can bring many to a knowledge of the truth (see D&C 6:11).

Through prayer, the Lord's Spirit will be poured out on us, and we will receive blessings greater than the treasures of the earth (see D&C 19:38).

If we are humble, the Lord will answer our prayers (see D&C 112:10).

We need to be submissive, gentle, patient, and long-suffering (see Alma 7:22–24).

Be like Nephi: Plead with the Lord to overcome your weaknesses (see 2 Nephi 4:16–31).

Be like Enos: Pour out your whole soul, with many long strugglings; pray and labor with all diligence (see Enos 1:1–12).

Be like Alma: Wrestle with God in mighty prayer (see Alma 8:10).

Be like the Savior: Luke says in Gethsemane "he prayed more earnestly" (see Luke 22:44).

GETTING PAST CLICHÉ-LEVEL PRAYER: VAIN REPETITIONS

The Lord warned us against "vain repetitions" in prayer (see Matthew 6:7). Is there anything wrong with repetition? No, in fact God often teaches us through repetition. He continually teaches and reteaches all through the scriptures. And in the holiest classroom on earth, in the house of the Lord, the main method used is repetition. It is *vain* repetition that we are warned about.

Are the Latter-day Saints guilty of using vain repetitions? Consider the following standard clichés used in Latter-day Saint prayers:

> *"We're thankful for this day."*
> *"We're thankful for the building we have to meet in."*
> *"We're grateful for all our many blessings."*
> *"Bless those who aren't here this week that they'll be
> here next week."*

"Bless the sick and afflicted."
"Bless us that no harm or accident will befall us."
"Bless us with all the blessings we stand in need of."
*"Bless the missionaries that they'll be guided to the
    honest in heart."*
*"Bless us that we'll strive to incorporate these things
    into our daily lives."*
"Take us all home in peace and safety."

Do we use clichés or vain repetitions? "Beyond a shadow of a doubt"!

Did you know that the Utah State Prison (and other states' prisons, too) has a chapel where religious meetings are held? When prisoners are released and return to normal society they have to make their lives work in a new way, and the gospel of Jesus Christ helps immensely. Therefore, as a Church we try to facilitate their reintegration into society in every good way possible. But can you imagine those prisoners standing up to pray in their church meetings on prison grounds and saying some of the same things we habitually say:

"We're thankful for the building we have to meet in."
*"Bless those who aren't here this week that they'll be
    here next week."*
"Take us all home in peace and safety."

Of course they wouldn't utter those expressions, because they don't apply to their situation.

Now, is there anything inherently wrong with saying any of the above phrases? Absolutely not—*as long as it is sincere, genuine, and heartfelt.* If we will, we can pray, even a long prayer, without "multiplying words" (see 3 Nephi 19:24). Heavenly Father knows what we are grateful for and what we need before we even kneel down. He does not necessarily need to hear it, but we need to say it. We need to express ourselves to him verbally—frequently and regularly. But we should do it from our hearts.

Besides the Savior and his prophets, who may be our best examples of how to pray? Children. Little children (before they become older and learn to imitate the way adults pray) are generally inclined to say whatever comes into their mind. They seem to say whatever they think or feel. Often their prayers are very revealing. Sometimes they are funny.

I don't remember too many missionary experiences from my first mission decades ago in Argentina, but I do remember kneeling one day with my companion in a humble little home with a family. The father was gone, as I recall, doing his job, delivering medications to doctors and dentists. He was traveling in the family's new car. We called on a little girl to say the prayer. She started out saying some of the usual things: "Heavenly Father, bless Mommy and Daddy; bless Granny and Grandpa." Then she said, "And bless our new Fiat." My companion and I had a hard time muffling a laugh. "Bless our new Fiat," I thought—you don't say something like that in a prayer! Well, since then I have wondered, why not? Is there anything wrong with asking Heavenly Father to bless your car? (Especially a Fiat!) That new little car meant much to that poor family; it was a necessity for providing their livelihood. Certainly it is not wrong in the sight of God to ask for anything we sincerely feel we need.

Maybe you have heard about the little boy who knelt down with his father beside the boy's bed. The father asked his son to offer the prayer. Several minutes went by—total silence. Finally the little boy got up, climbed into bed, pulled up the covers, and closed his eyes. His father interrupted, "I thought you were going to say the prayer."

"I did."

"Well, I didn't hear anything."

"I wasn't talking to you!"

Small children can indeed talk with Heavenly Father, and

they often say just whatever comes into their minds and hearts.

I always loved kneeling down and praying with my daughter Elizabeth when she was a toddler and a little girl. She was a creative thinker, and highly unusual remarks sometimes slipped into her prayers. She always prayed in a manner that was different from any other child I had ever heard. (We never had to worry about the old familiar clichés with Elizabeth!) I frankly enjoyed kneeling with her over those tender years, just to listen in on her conversations with Heavenly Father. In family prayer one day she asked Heavenly Father to "bless the missionaries in the MTC and out on missions to bring people to the true Church and not the great and abominable church." (So she had been listening in our Book of Mormon study after all!) . . . "Bless us all to pay our full tithes." . . . "Help us to make it through the deepest darkest tunnel, or in other words, the hardest times of our lives." (I don't know where she picked up that colorful figurative language, but her mother and I did have a hard time composing ourselves after the amen.)

It would probably do us all good to follow the example of little children and not get stuck in certain patterns of expression, but pray from our hearts.

WHAT LANGUAGE TO USE IN MIGHTY PRAYER

We believe that prayer follows four basic steps: We address our Heavenly Father—not the "Lord," as that term in common Latter-day Saint usage refers to the second member of the Godhead, our Savior, and we are not praying to him; we are praying to our Father in the Savior's name. We address the Father in a reverent, respectful tone (as we hear him addressed in the holy temple, for example). Then we thank him for the blessings we enjoy. We ask for those things we feel we need. And finally, we close in the name of Jesus Christ, and say "Amen."

We also use the language of prayer: pronouns such as *thee, thou, thy,* and *thine.* Our leaders have taught us that those terms constitute a reverential way of speaking with our Father in Heaven—different from the way we talk with anyone else. Those who know various world languages could point out that in some languages the pronouns we use in prayer are the formal manner of speaking to someone, while other languages use the informal terms. We don't speak as we do in prayer because of linguistics; we're simply following the pattern we have been taught to use, in English, when speaking with our Father.

Some people come into the Church from other churches and are accustomed to using *you* and *your*. Is that a sin? Certainly not, but we are encouraged to learn as quickly as possible the proper form of address in prayer. And these forms are not easy at times. We say, "you can" but, in prayer, "thou canst"; "you will" but, in prayer, "thou wilt"; "you do" but, in prayer, "thou doest" or "thou dost." So it does take some practice. If you are not acquainted with those forms, how do you learn them? From practice, listening to others pray who do use the correct form, and from studying the scriptures—that is the language of our King James Bible and the scriptures of the Restoration.

What Is "Mighty Prayer"?

There is a difference between "saying prayers" and really communicating with Heavenly Father. What do the scriptures mean when they speak of "pouring out your soul" to God? And when the scriptures refer to "mighty prayer," how does it happen?

Here are two illustrations from my own experience. During the mission in Santiago, Chile, I found myself frequently in the office staring at the picture board that contained two hundred photos of elders and sisters, with essential notes about their time in the mission and where they were presently serving. I spent a lot of time on my knees in that office, pleading with Heavenly Father for guidance in doing the work of his Son. A number of times I would be praying and I would actually open my eyes, get up off my knees, and stand before that picture board—still during my prayer—and pray for each missionary, by name. (That would take quite a while.) I wanted to look into the face of each and every missionary, mention their names, and ask for blessings on each one of them.

We need to get much more specific in our prayers, mentioning the names of people we know with special needs. They are all around us, in every ward, on every street. The Spirit will tell us for whom we can pray, and how we can help them.

Another example: Revelation often comes during prayer, and I know the limits of my memory. When the Lord tells me something, when he gives me some insight into a gospel principle or instruction about how to proceed with something or how to help someone, I need to write it down—not waiting until the end of my prayer or else I might forget it. So while I am still praying I will on occasion get up and grab a notebook and pen and record what came into my mind—even if it takes five or ten minutes to write about it (during which time even more revelation may come). Then I will get back on my knees and resume my prayer. Is that heresy—to get up and interrupt the flow of a prayer? To me, that is part of talking with my Father in Heaven. It is not a one-way monologue; it is two-way communication. If he tells me something, I need to write it down, right then.

I learned beautiful new truths recently as I studied the Gospels in the New Testament—at least to me they were new truths, and they brought some real doctrinal joy to me. They had a lot to do with a new vocabulary word: *importune.*

In the first eight verses of Luke 11 it is recorded that the disciples asked Jesus how to pray. He not only gave them a model prayer but taught them through a parable to seek God—as the friend at midnight—with "importunity." The active verb *importune* means "to request with urgency; to press with solicitation; to urge with frequent or unceasing application."[1] Jesus' story relates how a guest dropped in on a man in the middle of the night and the surprised host realized he had no food to offer his guest at that hour, so he attempted to wake up his sleeping neighbor to borrow three loaves of bread. The neighbor, though a friend, was reluctant to arise at that hour, but finally—because of persistent knock-ing—got up to answer the need. The main point of this parable is the importance of importuning—persisting in imploring for what we want from God. The parable is fol-lowed by the frequently quoted injunction: "Knock, and it shall be opened unto you . . . ; and to him that knocketh it shall be opened" (vv. 9–10). God wants us to pray, plead, implore, and *importune*—specifically, frequently, and sin-cerely. He wants us to ask.

I have noticed that Doctrine and Covenants 6 contains a host of phrases that urge us to desire and ask:

"if you will ask of me you shall receive" (v. 5)

"even as you desire of me so it shall be unto you" (v. 8)

"if thou wilt inquire, thou shalt know" (v. 11)

"as often as thou hast inquired thou hast received" (v. 14)

"I have spoken unto thee because of thy desires" (v. 20)

"I grant unto you . . . if you desire of me" (v. 25)

"if you have good desires . . ." (v. 27)

"Look unto me in every thought; doubt not, fear not" (v. 36)

The parable of the friend at midnight actually begins in the Joseph Smith Translation with a simple but powerful promise: "Your heavenly Father will not fail to give unto you whatsoever ye ask of him" (JST Luke 11:5). The message is: don't give up or despair; keep asking. Someone who learns to righteously importune is learning a key element in mighty prayer.

Not so long ago I realized that my prayer-life was changing. I had always been one to pray regularly and faithfully—though somewhat mechanically. I had experienced mighty prayer only intermittently. It came to me one day, like a quiet thunderbolt: I need to pray more often. I need to get on my knees more often. This mortal life, to stay on track, requires constant revelation. Better than "talking to" him is "communing with" him. The pressures in life can become almost overbearing, and we need direction. We need to hear the voice of the Lord speaking to us.

It is interesting that in a way I have always felt uncomfortable spending too much time on my knees, just talking, because I am a person who believes in being "up and doing." But I have learned that I have to be more humble and remember my own nothingness. With all my "up and doing," very little will happen without him. He can make things happen in an instant, if his servant will always avoid being "high and lifted up" and stay down in the depths of humility.

Two key questions to ask are: "Who can I help?" and "How can I help them?" Asking those questions, and diligently responding to heaven's answers to those questions, will help you secure a permanent relationship with your Father, your Savior, and the Holy Spirit.

Our first grandson started walking at ten months. During the first few days we saw him toddling down the hall of our home, he was able to keep his balance only by holding his two arms straight up in the air. As I watched him with loving delight, I realized he could stay on his feet and avoid falling only by keeping those arms pointed up, and I saw in his motion a beautiful gospel lesson: we, too, must symbolically keep our arms pointing upward in order to maintain our balance in this precarious earth life far from our heavenly home. To avoid a nasty fall, we keep extending our arms toward heaven, and open up our conversations—in mighty prayer— with a loving Father who will take our hand and keep us safe.

3

HOW TO HAVE MIGHTY FAITH

I HAVE NOTICED SEVERAL CURIOUS expressions in the scriptures: "mighty faith," the "eye of faith," the "prayer of faith," and "learning by faith." What do all these provocative phrases mean? And how can we come to understand this first principle of the gospel, faith, and use it more effectively? I believe examples of these concepts in the scriptures can help us immensely as we seek to answer these questions.

Alma told us that Melchizedek reigned over a people who had "waxed strong in iniquity and abomination; yea, they had all gone astray; they were full of all manner of wickedness" (Alma 13:17); yet later we learn that he was able to turn that gross wickedness around and help his people become so righteous that they didn't need to remain on earth any longer—

they were translated to join the people of Enoch (see JST Genesis 14:32–34).

I want to know what kind of home teacher Melchizedek was! What in the world did he do to so dramatically change the wicked disposition of his people? The next verse in Alma tells us: "Melchizedek having exercised mighty faith, and received the office of the high priesthood according to the holy order of God, did preach repentance unto his people. And behold, they did repent; and Melchizedek did establish peace in the land in his days" (Alma 13:18). So he used two of the greatest powers we know in the universe, faith and priesthood, to go out and preach repentance. And he was successful. But our question remains: what is this "mighty faith" and how did he get it and use it? We hope to answer that question in this chapter.

In his great discourse in the land of Zarahemla, Alma asked at least fifty questions. Among those questions were these: "Do ye exercise faith in the redemption of him who created you? Do you look forward with an eye of faith, and view this mortal body raised in immortality . . . to stand before God[?] . . . Can you imagine to yourselves that ye hear the voice of the Lord, saying unto you, in that day: Come unto me ye blessed, for behold, your works have been the works of righteousness upon the face of the earth?" (Alma 5:15–16). Alma talked about the "eye of faith," which enables us to visualize in our minds things we hope will happen. He knew that whatever we can vividly imagine, whatever we can see happening in our mind's eye, we can achieve, if it is the will of the Lord. When our eye of faith sees it happening, it will motivate us to literally move in that direction. As the Lord said in modern revelation, "According to your desires, yea, even according to your faith shall it be done unto you" (D&C 11:17).

When we envision our future standing before God in a fully repentant, blameless condition, our prayers become focused on that objective, and the Spirit enters our minds and hearts and constantly pushes us in the direction of fulfilling that noble purpose. "And the Spirit shall be given unto you by the prayer of faith" (D&C 42:14).

Mighty faith includes knowledge of godly things (we don't have a perfect knowledge, but we do know something); we have a surety; and we persevere, even in the face of adversity, because we believe the promises of the Lord. And we trust that the Lord will sustain us even though we are sometimes weak and vacillating.

I really like a statement made by a father who brought his son to be healed by Jesus. The Savior asked the father if he had faith to see his son healed, and the father replied, "Lord, I believe; help thou mine unbelief" (Mark 9:24). It is the same with all of us: we believe to a point; we do have faith to a degree, but we need the Lord to help us reach the 100 percent level required for the miracles. And he will help.

Doctrine and Covenants 88:118 says: "And as all have not faith [that is the truth, so what can we do to increase it?], seek ye diligently and teach one another words of wisdom; yea, seek ye out of the best books [the very best books are the scriptures] words of wisdom; seek learning, even by study and also by faith." So we seek learning by studying things out and by exercising faith. The greatest learning of all comes from heavenly sources. We ask in faith; we receive. In the process we receive more faith.

As we look back on the provocative phrases we noted in the above paragraphs, we can see a pattern in the Lord's instructions to us. Mighty faith—think it. The eye of faith—see it. The prayer of faith—say it. And learning by faith—seek it. Now let's examine specifically how we acquire this mighty faith.

THE ROLE OF *DESIRE*

Our faith may be measured by the amount of time we spend thinking about what we desire (refer back to the Lord's comments in Doctrine and Covenants 6 about our desires, as listed in chapter two)—because we get what we ask for. The Lord gives us what we truly want most—especially when we want what the Lord wants. Moroni wrote, "I know that thou workest unto the children of men according to their faith; . . . wherefore thou workest *after* men have faith" (Ether 12:29–30; emphasis added).

THE ROLE OF *WORKS*

Our faith may be measured by the effort we spend on obtaining our desire. I always told the missionaries I presided over that if you are not sure how much faith you have, just get out there and get to work—then you will see how much faith you have. You show your faith by your works. That is what James taught, and he illustrated it with the example of the great patriarch Abraham: "Was not Abraham our father justified by works, when he had offered Isaac his son upon the altar? Seest thou how faith wrought with his works, and *by works was faith made perfect?* And the scripture was fulfilled which saith, Abraham believed God, and it was imputed unto him for righteousness. . . . Ye see then how that by works a man is justified, and not by faith only" (James 2:21–24; emphasis added).

One day Jesus was journeying through Samaria and encountered ten lepers, who cried out for divine help (see Luke 17:11–19). The Savior instructed them simply to go show themselves to the priests, a requirement in the process of discerning and controlling leprosy in the old Mosaic law (see Leviticus 13:49).

Sometimes miraculous blessings come to those who simply follow instructions and keep a commandment. As the lepers were obedient they were healed. One of the ten, a Samaritan, returned to give thanks. He went back to Jesus to pour out his soul in gratitude to him who made his decaying flesh whole. All ten were obedient, and all ten received an immediate and extraordinary blessing for their obedience, but one wanted both to obey and to give thanks. This one leper was reminded that Jesus Christ had indeed cleansed him, but it was also the Samaritan's faith in Jesus Christ, along with his works, that made him whole.

We may feel that we want faith to *move* mountains, but sometimes we seem to lack the faith to *climb* those same mountains. President Kimball used to say, "If there's a mountain I need to climb, give me this mountain!"[1]

THE ROLE OF *SACRIFICE*

To exercise mighty faith we must be willing to sacrifice, to give up anything the Lord may require of us. The Prophet Joseph Smith wrote: "A religion that does not require the sacrifice of all things never has power sufficient to produce the faith necessary unto life and salvation; . . . the faith necessary unto the enjoyment of life and salvation never could be obtained without the sacrifice of all earthly things."[2] We may not literally have to give up all our earthly possessions (I think the Lord does want us to enjoy many beautiful things he has placed on this earth), but we have to be *willing* to sacrifice whatever the Lord may ask. Abraham, Lehi, and modern missionaries are examples of that: when they are called by the Lord to do so, they leave behind every person and every thing they have ever known, and they go anywhere the Lord sends them. "If God called me to walk back to Jackson County, for sure I'd go," we exclaim; but he is not calling us to go to Missouri—he is calling us to go a block or two and do our home teaching (or our visiting teaching). The sacrifices he requires of us, for our own good, include taking the time to pray and study the scriptures, giving up food and drink to fulfill the wonderful law of the fast, giving up time for our own pleasures to go to the temple and serve others. These works, along with many others, show our faith.

THE ROLE OF *OBEDIENCE*

A few weeks after we arrived to preside over the Chile Santiago East Mission, Sister Ogden and I met in the front room of our home to bid farewell to a group of missionaries who had completed their mission. One of those going home, Elder Fuller, bore his testimony and explained that he had had to make one of the hardest decisions of his mission during the previous week. He had planned to go back and visit a number of families and individuals he had taught and baptized in other parts of our mission, and in neighboring missions. But after the area president laid down the law and instructed missionaries not to return to old areas for farewell gatherings, he decided to obey. Because of that decision, as he related, the Lord blessed him and his companion with a wonderful investigator family, and that very night, just an hour before dashing off to the airport for the flight home, they saw that family dressed in white and baptized into the Church. They kept the rules with exactness and the Lord blessed them with a family to baptize. Eleven months later I learned that the family Elder Fuller baptized was a bulwark to their ward.

The wife was the Relief Society president, and the husband was first counselor in the bishopric.

When you have faith in the Lord and in his earthly leaders, and keep all the rules with exactness, rewards are plentiful. According to the scriptures, the results of mighty faith are mighty miracles: "God has provided a means that man, through faith, might work mighty miracles; therefore he becometh a great benefit to his fellow beings" (Mosiah 8:18). Ammon boasted in the Lord, as he said, "for in his strength I can do all things; yea, behold, many mighty miracles we have wrought in this land, for which we will praise his name forever" (Alma 26:12).

Mighty faith can also result in mighty changes. Describing what happened to his father, Alma the Younger said: "According to his faith there was a mighty change wrought in his heart. . . . And behold, he preached the word unto your fathers, and a mighty change was also wrought in their hearts, and they humbled themselves and put their trust in the true and living God. And behold, they were faithful until the end; therefore they were saved. And now behold, I ask of you, my brethren of the church, have ye . . . experienced this mighty change in your hearts?" (Alma 5:12–14).

A missionary wrote to me: "A man we recently baptized

had a wife who wanted nothing to do with us. We shared Alma 17:11 with him, told him to be an example, and pray for her. We found out later that they started praying together, and the other day, while her husband was receiving his baptismal interview, she asked to be baptized, too."

Through faith, she had experienced a change of heart.

EXAMPLES IN THE SCRIPTURES

The Savior has spent considerable effort over the centuries providing us with examples of mighty faith. He has had his prophets preserve these accounts so we can have superb illustrations of how to get it and use it.

Nephi, son of Lehi, is one of our models, one of our scriptural heroes that we can emulate. President Heber J. Grant once wrote: "I read the Book of Mormon as a young man, and fell in love with Nephi more than with any other character in [secular] or sacred history that I have ever read of, except the Savior of the world. No other individual has made such a strong impression upon me as did Nephi. He has been one of the guiding stars of my life."[3] Let's examine the first chapters of the Book of Mormon and learn about mighty faith from Nephi. Watch for the word *faith* in his record.

At the end of the first chapter of Nephi's writings he tells us: "I, Nephi, will show unto you that the tender mercies of the Lord are over all those whom he hath chosen, because of their faith, to make them mighty even unto the power of deliverance" (1 Nephi 1:20).

He goes on to relate to us how he came to believe God and be faithful to him: "Having great desires to know of the mysteries of God, wherefore, I did cry unto the Lord; and behold he did visit me, and did soften my heart that I did believe all the words which had been spoken by my father; wherefore, I did not rebel against him like unto my brothers. . . . And it came to pass that the Lord spake unto me, saying: Blessed art thou, Nephi, because of thy faith, for thou hast sought me diligently, with lowliness of heart" (1 Nephi 2:16, 19).

Chapter 3 of 1 Nephi gives the account of the Lord's command to Lehi to have his sons return to Jerusalem, after they had journeyed over two hundred miles through the desert. The message came to Lehi that the scriptural record on the plates of brass (containing much of what we call the Old Testament, plus more) was important enough to risk his sons' lives to obtain. It was essential that they take scriptures with them on their journey, to study them and live by them. We might ask at this point, Why did the Lord wait until they were more than two hundred miles away from Jerusalem to command Lehi to get the plates? Couldn't arrangements have been made for them before they left Jerusalem? It was a test of their faith.

Nephi's two older brothers complained and resisted, saying that it was a hard thing that Lehi, or even the Lord, was requiring of them. I know from personal experience that it was indeed a hard thing. In the late 1980s, accompanied by students and faculty from various Brigham Young University study groups, I walked the full distance from Jerusalem to the Red Sea, and I testify that it is some of the most desolate terrain on the surface of the earth, especially from the Dead Sea to the Red Sea, in the great Rift Valley.

An agreeable pace for a group of people would be between twenty and twenty-five miles a day. So the journey would have taken a minimum of eight days. Add to that the three days they journeyed after reaching the Red Sea, and it appears they traveled at least 250 miles in eleven or maybe twelve days. That measures one direction only. The round trip that the Lord and Father Lehi were asking of the four sons was over 500 miles, which would have taken at least three weeks through some of the most rugged terrain in the Near East.

And they had no clue as to how they were going to

obtain the plates. Further, we, having the advantage of knowing the end of this story from the beginning, are amazed to think ahead and realize that Lehi, soon after his sons returned from this assignment, would command them to go back again. One more test of faith. That is over a thousand miles and many weeks on those desolate tracts of land—and we have often looked critically at Laman and Lemuel for being chronic complainers.

Having already worked things out with the Lord, Nephi responded positively to the Lord's command. In one of the most inspiring outpourings of faith in all of scripture, Nephi assured his father that he would go and do the things the Lord had commanded because he knew that the Lord never gives a command without providing some way to fulfill it (see 1 Nephi 3:7). A believing attitude is a characteristic of every great soul. "As the Lord liveth, and as we live, we will not go down unto our father in the wilderness until we have accomplished the thing which the Lord hath commanded us" (1 Nephi 3:15). Nephi admitted that he didn't know exactly what they were going to do, but he had faith that the Lord would provide: "I was led by the Spirit, not knowing beforehand the things which I should do" (1 Nephi 4:6). The Lord did provide. He guided Nephi to take a route that took him to a drunken Laban, and then directed Nephi to take Laban's life and then to obtain the plates. Again, when we have faith and are exactly obedient, we are blessed with positive results—if not immediately, at least eventually.

Nephi admonished his brothers: "How is it that ye have forgotten that the Lord is able to do all things according to his will, for the children of men, if it so be that they exercise faith in him? Wherefore, let us be faithful to him" (1 Nephi 7:12).

Later, after all the travels back and forth, Nephi was carried away in the Spirit and had great visions of the future opened up to him (see 1 Nephi 11–14). Coming back down from the glories of those visions, he found his brothers murmuring and disputing, and he "spake many great things unto them, which were hard to be understood, save a man should inquire of the Lord; and they being hard in their hearts, therefore they did not look unto the Lord as they ought" (1 Nephi 15:3). Nephi chastised his brothers for not understanding and asked them, "Have ye inquired of the Lord? And they said unto me: We have not; for the Lord maketh no such thing known unto us" (1 Nephi 15:8–9). Of course the Lord couldn't help them understand, with that attitude.

Nephi counseled them again, and he gave us a masterful summary of what mighty faith is and how to get it: "Do ye not remember the things which the Lord hath said?—If ye will not harden your hearts, and ask me in faith, believing that ye shall receive, with diligence in keeping my commandments, surely these things shall be made known unto you" (1 Nephi 15:11).

Avoiding Discouragement

It is clear from Nephi's example that we have to maintain a positive attitude. We must avoid becoming discouraged, because a discouraged person is a weak person, and Satan can work on that weaker person more easily. And how do you avoid getting discouraged? "Trust in the Lord with all thine heart; and lean not unto thine own understanding. In all thy ways acknowledge him, and he shall direct thy paths" (Proverbs 3:5–6).

President Gordon B. Hinckley has provided a perfect example of a positive person, a perennial optimist. One of his favorite admonitions is "Don't be a pickle-sucker!"[4] And the title of the biography about his life is, understandably, *Go Forward with Faith.*

By our door at home we have a little laminated card with President Hinckley's picture and his words: "Be believing. Be happy. Don't get discouraged. Things will work out."[5] Is that just "hype"? No, it is the pure and simple truth. How can he say that? Because he has "the big picture." And how can we get the big picture? Through sincere prayer, studying the Savior's words, and exercising faith in them—believing that they are true and that it really is the best way to live—and asking him for a witness. He is glad to accommodate such requests.

Are you struggling right now and maybe doubting the Lord, or doubting yourself? Remember that questioning is fine, but doubt is spiritual poison. We are on a winning team; in the end this cause will triumph. Therefore, no matter what happens, don't quit the team! Go forward with faith. Your faith can make you whole. Your faith can also make others whole.

One more question: Why do we have to have so many *trials* of our faith? All I can say is—welcome to mortality! That is what this life is all about. We must be tested, tried, and proved to see what we are made of, to see if we are determined at all costs to learn of our Heavenly Father's lifestyle and to live it. And our trials are custom made, testing each individual according to what our omniscient Father knows we need in order to polish off the rough edges of our personalities. Of those who prove themselves worthy through all trials, the Savior has said: "I will own them, and they shall be mine in that day when I shall come to make up my jewels. Therefore, they must needs be chastened and tried, even as Abraham, who was commanded to offer up his only son. For all those who will not endure chastening, but deny me, cannot be sanctified" (D&C 101:3–5).

If we understood perfectly well just what was happening to us, and why it was happening, it would not be the same kind of trial. The purpose of the trial often needs to be almost incomprehensible to us while it's happening (though great understanding can come afterwards). Robert Frost penned some insightful lines depicting a conversation between the Lord and Job. It is not completely accurate as doctrine, but still we may learn from it. We will jump right into the middle of their conversation, as Frost imagined it. Here is the Lord speaking to Job:

> *I've had you on my mind a thousand years*
> *To thank you someday for the way you helped me*
> *Establish once for all the principle*
> *There's no connection man can reason out*
> *Between his just deserts and what he gets.*
> *Virtue may fail and wickedness succeed.*
> *'Twas a great demonstration we put on.*
> *I should have spoken sooner had I found*
> *The word I wanted. You would have supposed*

One who in the beginning was *the Word*
Would be in a position to command it. . . .
Too long I've owed you this apology
For the apparently unmeaning sorrow
You were afflicted with in those old days.
But it was of the essence of the trial
You shouldn't understand it at the time.
It had to seem unmeaning to have meaning.
And it came out all right.[6]

Indeed, things will always turn out all right in the end for those who love and trust the Lord. No wonder faith is listed as the first principle of the gospel. It comes first and makes everything else work.

4

HOW TO ENJOY MIGHTY REPENTANCE

THERE IS SCARCELY ANY PRINCIPLE OF THE gospel more important than repentance. At least that is what the Lord seems to be saying in the scriptures. If you look at Doctrine and Covenants 15 or 16 (they are both the same revelation; one addressed to a man named Peter, the other to a man named John—last name of both: Whitmer), you will notice that one significant question is answered: the thing that would be of most worth to them is to declare repentance to the people (verse 6 in each section). In fact, the Lord himself several times instructed his servants to "say nothing but repentance unto this generation" (D&C 6:9; 11:9; see also 19:21). Does he mean that literally? Is every topic of all missionary discussions supposed to be repentance? Must repentance be the subject of every Church classroom discussion? Of course not. Why did he say it that way, then? The Lord was using, as he did in his mortal ministry, a figure of speech called hyperbole, which is an intentional exaggeration to emphasize a point. He said it in a hyperbolic way to stress the fact that there is nothing more important in all the gospel than to get people to repent. This one principle is so vital that it towers above others in primacy and urgency. Driven by faith, repentance is an essential principle to live in order to make the Savior's atonement effective and meaningful in our life.

The Greek verb "to repent" is *metanoi,* meaning to change one's mind, to reconsider. The Hebrew verb "to repent" is *lashuv,* meaning to return, to come back (to God). In fact, we find both terms, "repent" and "return," together in a number of passages. For example, in the famous remark in Alma 34:34 we read, "Ye cannot say, when ye are brought to that awful crisis, that I will *repent,* that I will *return* to my God" (emphasis added).

Repentance is a sincere return, a reconciliation with our Heavenly Father. It is not just feeling guilty for having sinned, nor is it mere "forgetfulness," pushing the sin way back in our minds to conveniently not be reminded of it. In true repentance, confession is only a start. It is an attitude change and a behavior change. We repent not only of sins, but *of sinning,* and we are willing to do whatever is necessary to remove the stain and the pain. We turn to the Savior. He is the only one who can take away our sins, because he paid the price. All other methods of "self-improvement" (positive mental attitude seminars, tapes, books, etc.) are terrestrial. The Lord's celestial system for making things right in our lives is repentance.

A Study of Repentance

Years ago I wanted to study everything the Lord has said about repentance in the scriptures. I knew it would be a big job, because he has said a lot about this subject. I delayed it for quite some time but finally studied the hundreds of passages and organized my study in outline form. Over the years, in almost every course I teach, I have given a copy of that repentance study to numerous students, so they, too, can learn from the Lord's words. It has proved to be the single most valuable assignment I have ever given. (You will find a copy of that repentance study in the appendixes of this book under the title, "What the Lord Says about Repentance.")

In my study I saw clearly that repentance is a commandment and that its purpose is the remission of sins. If you wonder if you have properly repented of your sins and had them remitted (that is, permanently erased), then you can review the scriptural pattern, given below, and answer for yourself.

Godly Sorrow and Suffering Are Necessary

According to the scriptures, if you haven't suffered, you haven't repented. We have all been through the anguish; sometimes we feel like pounding our head against the wall, and we wonder how we could be so foolish as to do the sinful things we do. We hurt inside. And it is not just guilt for being caught or feeling the embarrassment for having to confess. It is godly sorrow we are feeling (see 2 Corinthians 7:10).

President Ezra Taft Benson said: "Sometimes we regard all too lightly the principle of repentance, thinking that it only means confession, that it only means feeling sorry for ourselves. But it is more than that. It is a deep, burning, and heartfelt sorrow for sin that will drive us to our knees in humility and tears—a deep, heartfelt sorrow for sin that produces a reformation of life."[1]

At the end of 1995 the dermatologist told me I had some cancerous cells in the side of my nose. Therefore, in January and February of 1996 I was willing to go through cancer treatments (twenty-five radiation treatments and then application of a chemotherapeutic cream) for a one-month period, to remove all the potentially life-threatening cells. The first couple of weeks were easy and hardly any effects of the treatments were noticeable, but then about the third week my skin began to dry up and get very tight; large, bright-red pustules appeared where the treatments had been concentrated. At that point the treatments became extremely uncomfortable and bothersome, but I was willing to go through it all to cleanse my face and burn out all the deadly cells so they wouldn't kill me.

Repentance is like those treatments. We are willing to go through some minor discomfort— the godly sorrow and suffering required of us personally—so that those sins cannot eventually kill us spiritually.

Years ago I saw a painting called "Four Faces of Repentance" in an old *Instructor* magazine. It made quite an impression on me. A similar illustration is reproduced here to portray the stages we go through to be totally rid of our sins—from the agonizing pain of darkness to the glimmer of hope and recognition that there is a Light we can turn to; then from fully committing to dedicate ourselves to the Light of the world to being able once again to bask in the brilliant

The Four Faces of Repentance, by J. Bryant Ward (used by permission)

light of peace and joy—and to experience the forgiveness and love of God.

As we consider this illustration, we might also think of the individual in scripture who has given us the most detailed, most graphic portrayal of the pains of a damned soul—Alma the Younger. I am grateful that he was willing to divulge (and actually carve into the record) those intimate and agonizing details of what he went through to be forgiven of his sins. His vivid words and expressions are recorded in Mosiah 27:28–29 and in Alma 36:12–17.

Alma described wading through tribulation, bitterness, bonds, the abyss, and the inexpressible horror that accompanied the thought of having to stand before God and answer for all he had done. Alma wrote that he was "harrowed up" by the memory of his many sins. What is a harrow? Those involved in cultivating field crops know that it is an implement that is dragged behind an animal (and now behind a tractor) to break up the hard ground for planting. If a harrow were dragged over a live body, it would certainly become an instrument of torture. Alma also wrote that he was racked with torment. What is a rack? An instrument of torture. Alma chose his words intentionally; he was tortured by his sins, just as the man portrayed in the illustration.

Alma later taught his own wayward son, one who was sinning grievously while serving a mission: "Let your sins trouble you"—meaning what? Let his sins bother him to bring him down to severe depression? No. Alma said, "Let your sins trouble you, with that trouble which shall bring you down unto repentance" (Alma 42:29). We should be glad we can suffer the godly sorrow now so we won't have to suffer the full effects of our sins later.

Confession Is Necessary

Elder Spencer W. Kimball taught: "No one can ever be forgiven of any transgression until there is repentance, and one has not repented until he has bared his soul and admitted his intentions and weaknesses without excuses or rationalizations. He must admit to himself that he has grievously sinned. When he has confessed to himself without the slightest minimizing of the offense, or rationalizing its seriousness, or soft-pedaling its gravity, and admits it is as *big* as it really *is,* then he is ready to begin his repentance."[2]

We have a worry these days. Many in this generation seem to be growing up with the carefree attitude, "I can sin now, and I can always repent later; it only takes a few months of waiting and I can go on a mission, or I can go to the temple." But Elder Richard G. Scott warned: "The thought of intentionally committing serious sin now and repenting later is perilously wrong. . . . Premeditated sin has greater penalties and is harder to overcome."[3]

We must confess and forsake our sins now and not put off our repentance. Alma warned us not to procrastinate the day of our repentance. As the old rabbis used to say: "You cannot repent the day before you die, because you don't know what day you will die."

When we returned to Utah in the summer of 2000 after our mission in Chile, we found our oldest daughter dating a young man named McKell, a lively returned missionary who was also involved in theater programs at Brigham Young University. He was a fairly frequent visitor in our home, and we came to like him.

That fall our daughter was awakened one Sunday morning to hear some terrible news. Her friend McKell had been visiting a cousin along the coast of Oregon, and the two of them were far out on a pier when a storm came up suddenly and swept them off into the water. His cousin was battered among some rocks, rescued, and then rushed off to a hospital where he struggled for his life. McKell was apparently swept away by the undertow, and his body was not recovered. Eight days later, the very day of a memorial service for him in his home state, his body washed up onto the shore along Oregon's coast and could finally have a proper burial.

McKell was a good young man of twenty-five years, but I don't believe he knew he would be leaving the earth that day.

Sister Davidson was one of our extraordinary sister missionaries in Chile. When she finished her mission she returned to school at Brigham Young University and continued serving in her ward. One Sunday afternoon, while crossing the street near her apartment complex, she was struck by a car and killed. She was on her way to a meeting and suddenly found herself on the way to a different meeting. I spoke in a memorial service for her a few days later. I don't believe Sister Davidson knew she would be leaving the earth that day.

The fact is, none of us knows exactly when we will be departing this mortal sphere, so we should be ready always—never procrastinating the day of our repentance but repenting daily and keeping ourselves prepared to meet God.

While you are here on earth, don't wait to do your repenting until the pressure situations of mission and marriage arrive. If the announcements and invitations have already been sent out, and you then go to the interview with the bishop or a member of the stake presidency and realize you are not ready for the sacred covenant-making in the house of the Lord—then what do you do? It could be pretty embarrassing, couldn't it? Ultimately, however, the embarrassment doesn't matter; you don't ever want to enter the holy temple if you are not worthy. To take upon yourself the most sacred covenants and make the most binding promises of your whole life when you are not spiritually prepared or worthy to do so would bring upon you condemnation of terrifying proportions.

Before going to the temple, before going to sacrament meeting, even before kneeling to pray, seek to be reconciled to Heavenly Father and to the Savior, and seek to be reconciled to any brother or sister. If there is conflict or friction at all between you and another person, get it resolved now (see Jesus' counsel to that effect in Matthew 5:23–24).

Restitution Is Necessary

President Ezra Taft Benson was known to quip: "It is better to prepare and prevent than it is to repair and repent."[4] True. It is better not to commit sin in the first place than have to make reparations and go through the rest of the repentance process. But alas, we are all human and do make mistakes, so it is good we can make some compensation for that which is lost. The four rebellious and sinful sons of King Mosiah, as part of their full repentance, went out among the people and zealously strove to repair all injuries done (see Mosiah 27:35). Restitution, or making amends, restoring what was taken (as much as possible), is a vital part of true repentance.

Forsaking Is Necessary

"By this ye may know if a man repenteth of his sins— behold, he will confess them and forsake them" (D&C 58:43). To forsake means to give up, abandon, cease to do. Indeed, we must abandon all sin as soon as we can (and it might require a lengthy and mighty struggle to rid ourselves of our toughest and most perplexing weaknesses and inclinations). It is mandatory, as soon as possible, to expel sin and the propensity to sin from our lives. That is forsaking.

There is another angle for us to look at regarding the forsaking of sins. When I was first called to work with the missionaries at the Missionary Training Center in Provo, Utah, I quickly learned that most of the elders and sisters were truly prepared and worthy to be there. Those who were not soon found they couldn't learn the discussions; they couldn't learn to love their companion; nothing seemed to go right, because they couldn't get the Spirit; and they couldn't get the Spirit because they were not clean. Those few had to return home and repent (and then many of them were able to return to the MTC and make it work).

Although the great majority of the missionaries were indeed prepared and worthy to be there, I noticed that even among them there were some who found themselves agonizing over past sins. They had fully repented, but they still had a bright recollection of their recent (and sometimes distant) sins, and they became depressed as they remembered what they had done in their past. Why couldn't they move on? Because they had forsaken their sins in the sense that they stopped doing them; but in another sense they had not yet forsaken them. Part of forsaking is forgiving yourself and putting the sins behind you—burying the old man of sin, as the Apostle Paul put it (see Romans 6:3–8), leaving those sins buried, and not digging them up any more.

Sometimes people will sincerely desire to repent and secure Heavenly Father's complete forgiveness, saying to the Savior, "Here, Lord; here's my whole package of sin. Please take it away." And He does. Then we go back and say, "Wait a minute. Give me some of those sins back; I want to suffer a little more for them!" No. When you have totally repented, you must forsake those sins, forget about them, bury them away, and not bring them up again. Jesus beautifully stated the principle in agricultural terms: "No man, having put his hand to the plough, and looking back, is fit for the kingdom of God" (Luke 9:62). In other words, when you have planted your life in a more spiritual furrow, keep your eyes straight ahead and don't look back to the old sins, the old people, the old places. Someone has suggested that when Satan reminds you of your past, just remind him of his future! Keep your eyes looking ahead, and on the Savior.

I really like the words of the Prophet Isaiah: "Thou shalt forget the shame of thy youth" (Isaiah 54:4). I am taking those words out of their historical context, but I find the phrase itself profoundly meaningful. We all know that scarcely anyone gets through the teenage years these days unscathed. Everyone has problems growing up, some worse than others, but it is imperative that we forget the shame of our youth. Repent, put it behind you, and move on. Even Joseph Smith confessed that during his youth he struggled with "all kinds of temptations; and, mingling with all kinds of society, I frequently fell into many foolish errors, and displayed the weakness of youth, and the foibles of human nature; which, I am sorry to say, led me into divers temptations, offensive in the sight of God" (Joseph

Smith—History 1:28). He went on to explain that he was never guilty of any great or malignant sins—he was never disposed to commit such—but he did have to repent and put his indiscretions behind him. So did the Apostle Paul. He, too, had to dispose of a sinful past. He wrote to the Saints in Macedonia: "*Forgetting those things which are behind,* and reaching forth unto those things which are before, I press toward the mark for the prize of the high calling of God in Christ Jesus" (Philippians 3:13–14; emphasis added).

One sister missionary, while bearing her testimony during the first hours at the MTC, explained that she had experienced a long, hard struggle to prepare herself and be worthy to represent the Lord as a missionary. She didn't go into any detail of her past sins; she just let everyone know that she had gone through an extended period of serious repentance. But at one point in her testimony, she stopped, smiled, and said, "I can't even remember the person I used to be."

When you have fully repented of your sins and are converted to the Lord, you are born again—you become a new person. You don't have to be concerned about your old sins because that old person who committed those sins is buried away. That is not you. You have become a new person who would not commit such sins. Therefore, you can forgive yourself, forsake those sins, and forget your past. You are a new and different person.

After Repentance, Good Works Are Necessary

One day I sat at my computer working on a paper. By late afternoon I must have typed twelve to fourteen pages of original thinking. Then, after the full day's work, tired and ready to close everything down, I inadvertently trashed the document. I don't know what I was thinking, but I had lost many hours of work. As I sat agonizing over my loss, thinking ahead to the next day's work of trying to resurrect all those thoughts, and feeling miserable about having to do it all over again, a thought came to my mind: "Call your friend Jim." Jim was a computer troubleshooter; if there was a problem with computers, he could fix it. I called him, and he said my document was still there. "But no," I countered, "I trashed it and can't bring it back up." By that time I had turned off my computer and was about to leave for home. "It's still there," Jim repeated.

The next day, Jim came to my office with a collection of recovery programs in his hands. He tried one and nothing happened. My heart sank anew. He tried another, then I began to see paragraph after paragraph of my document appearing on the screen. My eyes grew bigger and my smile broader as I watched every paragraph of my writings reappear on my computer. I did have to reformat a little, but it was all there.

Jim taught me something: it is still there until you type over it. It is still there until you cover it over with something else. As I thought about that later, a wonderful gospel lesson came to mind. Now I wouldn't want anyone to take my analogy too far, but in a sense what I had experienced with my computer is like my sins—they are still there until I repent and cover them up with good works. That is what Jesus has done for us. The Hebrew word for atonement is *kippur* (as in Yom Kippur, the day of atonement), and the basic meaning of *kippur* is to cover up. The Savior has suffered for, and covered up, the sins of us all—pending our complete repentance.

Part of the full repentance process, then, involves your ongoing commitment to good works on behalf of others. It's another way you show Heavenly Father that you have truly repented and changed. And what are some of the good works you can do? Giving your best time, talents, and resources to the Lord and his work, daily prayer, scripture study, serving others, regular worship in the temple, fasting, avoiding temptations (including certain kinds of music, literature, movies, and Internet sites), and so on.

One of my former BYU students commented on his conversion and continual repentance: "I was raised in another Christian church and was taught that men are saved by faith and not works. I thought that baptism was all that was required to be reconciled with the Father. Somehow I knew that this must not be the full truth. I felt very out of touch with the Lord, and I knew that I needed more light. I was reading *The Miracle of Forgiveness* by Spencer W. Kimball when I learned what I was missing. One night I poured out my soul to Heavenly Father. I had been so afraid and confused. I was willing to do anything to follow his will for my life. After many hours of tears and heartfelt sorrow I committed to living his gospel. After telling my family and talking to a bishop, I was baptized and received the Holy Ghost.

"I will never forget the peace and joy I felt. I didn't care what I would face in trials or pain because I knew I had finally found what I had been seeking for so long.

"I know that repentance is a continual process. I have gotten off track and have been through even more sorrow than before. This was because I had made a covenant with the

Lord and I had become lazy in my commitment to the gospel."

President Spencer W. Kimball suggested that the most important word in the English language is the word *remember.* The Book of Mormon has a number of verses beginning: "O, remember, remember"! (Alma 37:13; Helaman 5:9; see also Mosiah 2:41; Helaman 5:12; 14:30). That is our problem: We seem to forget too quickly how much we owe the Lord; we become lazy in our commitment to the gospel; and our good works taper off. It takes constant effort to remember, but your daily prayers will help, as you ask Heavenly Father, "Who can I help?" and "How can I help them?"

Our Obligation to Forgive Others

Can you seriously expect Heavenly Father to forgive you of all your sins if you are holding out and refusing to forgive others?

Notice a serious warning the Lord issued to Latter-day Saints about a problem former-day Saints had: "My disciples, in days of old, sought occasion against one another and forgave not one another in their hearts; and for this evil they were afflicted and sorely chastened. Wherefore, I say unto you, that ye ought to forgive one another; for he that forgiveth not his brother his trespasses standeth condemned before the Lord; for there remaineth in him the greater sin. I, the Lord, will forgive whom I will forgive, but of you it is required to forgive all men" (D&C 64:8–10).

The Lord indicated that the sin of some ancient Saints lay in not forgiving others *in their hearts.* It is sometimes easy to pronounce the words, "I forgive you," without really meaning it deep in our hearts. There are a lot of offenses out there these days, and a lot of abuses, but we must come to an ability to forgive. That is a godlike quality we must acquire.

It is helpful if we work on *overcoming* the problems *we* have, and *overlooking* the problems *others* have.

CONSEQUENCES OF NOT REPENTING

The Book of Mormon prophet Jacob said, as "ye look upon me as a teacher, it must needs be expedient that I teach you the consequences of sin" (2 Nephi 9:48), "warning [you] against . . . every kind of sin [and] the *awful consequences* of them" (Jacob 3:12; emphasis added).

The scriptures are quite explicit about the awful consequences facing those who refuse to repent: "Except ye repent, ye shall . . . perish" (Luke 13:3). King Benjamin spoke of guilt, pain, anguish, and shrinking from God's presence (see

Mosiah 2:38). The unrepentant cannot be saved (see Alma 5:31, 51). Those who will not repent will have the light previously given to them taken away (see D&C 1:33). Repent, the Lord commands, or suffer (see D&C 19:4) and be cast out (see D&C 42:28).

REWARDS FOR REPENTING

Though the consequences for not repenting are most unpleasant, even dire, the rewards for repenting are most appealing, even stunning. The gospel of Jesus Christ is occasionally referred to in the scriptures as the gospel of repentance (see D&C 13:1; 138:57; Joseph Smith–History 1:69). The word *gospel* means "good news"; therefore, it is the good news of repentance. We sometimes look upon repentance as a punishment, as a distasteful, negative thing. It does involve some pain, of course, but genuine repentance is a blessing— a happy, positive thing.

Repentance brings remission of sins, peace of conscience, and joy (see Mosiah 4:3). Two questions are often asked: (1) How can you know if you have been forgiven of your sins? King Benjamin's answer, as indicated in the above passage, is that you will have peace of conscience. By that peace and the assurance of the Spirit you will know. (2) If the Lord says he will forgive and forget, why can't I forget? If I sit down and think about it, why can I still conjure up the lurid details of my past sins? The Lord leaves the memory in your mind as an early warning system; it is protection against going back to the old ways, the old sins. Alma didn't say he could remember his *sins* no more; he said he could remember his *pain* no more. He could remember his sins all right, but he was not harrowed up by the memory of those sins, because he had repented of them.

When you fully repent you are born again and become a new person (see Mosiah 27:24–29); you become a person who can know the mysteries of God, receive revelation, and bring souls to Christ (see Alma 26:22). The cloud of darkness that once overshadowed you is removed (see Helaman 5:41). You will continuously use the miracle of repentance, being relieved of the heavy burdens of sin, and eventually find yourself guiltless on your day of judgment (see 3 Nephi 27:16).

Whatever your past has been, your future is spotless; so tie yourself to your potential, not your past. One of the most beautiful truths of the plan of happiness is that the Lord forgives and forgets (see D&C 58:42). He chooses what he will remember. When we forsake "Babylon," God forgets we ever lived there.

Another question: What if you feel you have gone too far? That Heavenly Father would never allow you back? Isn't that exactly what the prodigal son felt? "Father, I have sinned against heaven, and before thee, and am no more worthy to be called thy son" (Luke 15:18–19).

Truman G. Madsen taught: "If there are here some of you who have been tricked into the conviction that you have gone too far, that you have been weighed down with doubts, . . . that you have had the poison of sin that makes it impossible ever again to be what you could have been—then hear me. I bear testimony that you cannot sink farther than the light and sweeping intelligence of Jesus Christ can reach. I bear testimony that as long as there is one spark of the will to repent and reach, *He is there.* He did not just descend *to* your condition; He descended *below* it."[5]

I know of a man in the scriptures who helped make images of false gods, yet he became the head of one of our priesthoods (Aaron). I know of two men who persecuted God's Church and were vile sinners, yet they had their calling and election made sure (Alma and Paul). I know of two men who used the word "wretched" to describe themselves, because of their sins (Nephi and Paul), yet they went on to become two of our most revered prophets. I know a young woman who committed adultery and came close to committing suicide; she honestly considered herself, as she said, the "most corrupt person in the world"; yet she thoroughly repented and found a wonderful man and later married in the temple.

Unless you have murdered someone (premeditated murder) or committed the sin against the Holy Ghost (as very few have), you can be totally forgiven of all of your sins. That is indeed good news. But you must ask! The Lord said, "Thy sins are forgiven thee, *according to thy petition*" (D&C 90:1; emphasis added).

One day, while working at my desk in BYU's Joseph Smith Building, I had to erase some writing at the top of some student assignments. I reached into a drawer where I keep a box of pencils that have erasers at the end. I grabbed one of the erasers and began vigorously erasing, and while I was erasing I admit that the smell brought back some nostalgic feelings. All through the years of growing up, just before elementary school began each year, I remember going out with my mother and buying school supplies: paper, notebooks, pencils, rulers, . . . and erasers. Erasers were always part of the "equipment of education." Having them was not seen as negative thinking; it was just a real part of learning—

we knew we would make mistakes and needed erasers. So is it with life. We knew we would come to earth, to this "education probation," and make mistakes. We need erasers, and fortunately, our mistakes are not written in ink, but in pencil, and can be totally erased.

One caution, however. The erasure—the repentance and forgiveness—doesn't usually come in the dramatic, "lightning and thunder" experiences. President Ezra Taft Benson wisely explained:

"We must be careful, as we seek to become more and more godlike, that we do not become discouraged and lose hope. Becoming Christlike is a lifetime pursuit and very often involves growth and change that is slow, almost imperceptible. The scriptures record remarkable accounts of men whose lives changed dramatically, in an instant, as it were: Alma the Younger, Paul on the road to Damascus, Enos praying far into the night, King Lamoni. Such astonishing examples of the power to change even those steeped in sin give confidence that the Atonement can reach even those deepest in despair.

"But we must be cautious as we discuss these remarkable examples. Though they are real and powerful, they are the exception more than the rule. For every Paul, for every Enos, and for every King Lamoni, there are hundreds and thousands of people who find the process of repentance much more subtle, much more imperceptible. Day by day they move closer to the Lord, little realizing they are building a godlike life. They live quiet lives of goodness, service, and commitment. . . .

"We must not lose hope. Hope is an anchor to the souls of men. Satan would have us cast away that anchor. In this way he can bring discouragement and surrender. But we must not lose hope. . . . We must remember that most repentance does not involve sensational or dramatic changes, but rather is a step-by-step, steady, and consistent movement toward godliness."[6]

A "COMPLETE CLEANSE" IS NEEDED

Now and then my wife and I find ourselves sitting alone at our kitchen table eating a meal and reading. We are both voracious readers; we always have a stack of reading material (newspaper, *Ensign, Reader's Digest, National Geographic,* or one of her many "health nut" publications). One day I was just thumbing through a magazine when a certain page caught my attention. Half the page showed a man with a serious look on his face, and superimposed on the picture was a question in big print: **ARE YOU CLEANSED?** That question particularly aroused my curiosity. I noticed that the page was an advertisement for a whole line of cleansing products: Adrenal Cleanse, Blood Cleanse, Heart Cleanse, Joint Cleanse, Kidney Cleanse, Liver Cleanse, and Prostate Cleanse. Then I noticed something that caught my attention even more. Just below the picture of the man was this sentence: "At last, a complete cleanse line from a name I can trust." Now, you might suspect how that sentence registered in my mind. Yes, I thought, I certainly do know about a "complete cleanse" that comes through a Name I can trust.

In Santiago, Chile, there are four ambulance companies in a large city of five to six million people. One of the companies is called *Rescate Total* ("Total Rescue"), and every time I saw one of their ambulances driving by I thought, No, I know where total rescue comes from. His name is Jesus Christ. And his is the only name under heaven whereby salvation comes, from whom a complete cleanse can come—because he is the One who paid the price. He is the only person in the universe who can take away all our transgressions.

THE BAPTISM OF REPENTANCE

The culmination of our repentance is the simple, beautiful ordinance of baptism. But that brief act of total immersion into water never has and never will take away anyone's sins. It is not the baptismal water that cleanses sin; it is the power of Jesus Christ and his atoning sacrifice. We partake of that power by receiving the ordinances he has prescribed, always coupled with faith, and, in the case of baptism, with repentance. Thus, faith in the Savior and his atoning sacrifice for us, combined with genuine repentance and baptism, fulfill our part of making that atonement work for us personally. Baptism is but a climax of the process that burns out and washes away all that is unclean and undesirable in us, removing the stain and the pain of our sins. Therefore, the phrase "baptism of repentance" is an appropriate combination of words indicating that baptism is the fulfillment, or the concluding act, of all our prior efforts to repent and return to God. The brief action of going down into and coming back up out of the waters of baptism is a manifestation of humility and submission on the part of a person to do exactly what the Lord requires. The ordinance is short in time but eternal in significance.

But is that all there is to it? Does the process end there? Can we never again be "baptized unto repentance" and have all our sins taken away?

Sometimes we look with envy at the new convert stepping out of the baptismal font; we feel almost jealous of the fact that he or she, for a time, is the cleanest, purest person on earth. "How would it be?" we wonder. "Oh, that I could be baptized again and be freed from all my sins!" The fact is that we can be freed from all our sins on a regular basis. If we go to sacrament meeting each week (the most sacred public meeting we have in the Church), and if we go having thoroughly repented of all our sins, then we worthily eat that little piece of bread and drink that little cup of water, *renewing the covenants we made at baptism.* By doing so, we can literally be clean and pure, totally void of sin, as we walk out of sacrament meeting each week. We can experience again and again the baptism of repentance.

IT IS MORE THAN A CLEANSE

Actually, the whole process of repentance accomplishes more than a "cleanse." Elder Dallin H. Oaks wrote: "We often think of the results of repentance as simply cleansing us from sin. That is an incomplete view of the matter. A person who sins is like a tree that bends easily in the wind. On a windy and rainy day the tree may bend so deeply against the ground that the leaves become soiled with mud, like sin. If we only focus on cleaning the leaves, the weakness in the tree that allowed it to bend and soil its leaves may remain. Merely cleansing the leaves does not strengthen the tree. Similarly, a person who is merely sorry to be soiled by sin will sin again in the next high wind. The susceptibility to repetition will continue until the tree has been strengthened.

"When a person has gone through the [full repentance process], the Savior not only cleanses that person from sin, he also gives him or her new strength. . . . To be admitted to [Heavenly Father's] presence, we must be more than clean. We must also be changed from a weak person who has transgressed into a strong person with the spiritual stature to dwell in the presence of God."[7]

He Can Repair All Damage Done

On March 1, 1998, my wife, Marcia, and I attended the conference of the Javiera Carrera Stake in Santiago, Chile. I bore testimony that Heavenly Father wants his children who have strayed to come back in the fold. We can repent and return. And I reminded the members that the last time Sister

Ogden and I spoke to them in that stake was just a few hours after I had wrecked our van. We had to get by without that vehicle for two and a half months while it was being repaired. But, I told them, if they wanted to see our van now, they could go right out in front of the Church and see it. And they could look closely, but they would not see any signs of it ever having been damaged, because it was beautifully and completely repaired. I bore testimony that our lives can be totally repaired also. The damage caused by the wreckage of sin can be repaired so that the damage cannot even be detected. The Savior can reactivate the Spirit in our lives. He can repair all damage done.

But as Elder Oaks explained, the atonement does even more than give us a cleanse and repair all damage done. Early in 1984, while returning to our home in Jerusalem, I must have been handling our large, heavy suitcases in such a way that something went wrong in my lower back. For several months I periodically found myself in excruciating pain, apparently from some bone fragments sticking into the largest nerve in my body, the sciatic nerve that runs down the spine and into the legs. After I had three months of experimental treatments in Israeli hospitals—and after I experienced three months of not being able to function because of the intense pain—my doctor put me on the strongest pain-killer he could prescribe without personally accompanying me and sent me on a plane flight across the world to Salt Lake City, for a back operation. The surgery was successful. After some weeks of recovery I flew back to the Holy Land to resume teaching and guiding the students on field-study trips all over the lands of the Bible.

I learned something from that painful ordeal. It is not enough to repair the damage done; I have to continually strengthen my back so it doesn't happen again. So it is with repentance: We must cleanse or purge ourselves of all that is wrong inside, repair the damage that has been done, and continually strengthen ourselves to become more and more resistant to sin and more and more capable of sustaining light and truth from Him who is our strength.

5

HOW TO GET AND KEEP THE SPIRIT

GARY, ONE OF MY HIGH SCHOOL FRIENDS, grew up to be a police officer. He is tall and funny. He used to tell me that he would pull someone over and arrest him for "being ugly in a public place." One day Gary said to me, very seriously, "People never change." And he repeated it: "People never change . . . *unless they're touched by the Holy Ghost.*"

For people to make mighty changes in their life, something has to happen inside. I saw it regularly while working with the missionaries. They would write to me that their investigators "felt something." Here are some direct quotes from missionaries' weekly reports (I have added the emphasis):

"My companion and I bore our testimony, testifying of the importance of baptism, and they recognized the Spirit;

one of them started to cry and said: 'I've never *felt* in any church what I *feel* now; it's something incredible and I can't describe it—a *feeling* so beautiful; it makes me want to cry. I'm going to be baptized!'"

"I know without a doubt . . . because I can *feel* it—something in my heart is *burning*."

"We gave him a Book of Mormon and invited him to read and pray. When we came back to follow up he told us that while he was reading he *felt* something—he is 'more at *peace*.'"

"A couple decided to be baptized. They have been members of four different churches. She said they *felt* something different in our testimony meeting she just couldn't explain."

Brigham Young, after receiving a copy of the Book of Mormon, studied it and investigated the Church for a year and a half. He was not impressed with the physical appearance or the intellectual ability of the missionaries of the Church, but he could not deny the truths they taught and the Spirit that accompanied their testimonies. He said, "The brethren who came to preach the Gospel to me, I could easily out-talk them, though I had never preached; but *their testimony was like fire in my bones*."[1]

That is exactly what Jeremiah experienced in Jerusalem.

For years he was out on the streets of Jerusalem calling on the people to repent, and it was not pleasant work. Some of the people became violent and abusive in their language and treatment of the prophet. "I am in derision daily, every one mocketh me," he exclaimed. Then he said, "I will not make mention of him, nor speak any more in his name"—he was not going to declare the word of the Lord to the people any more; he felt like quitting his mission. "But," he continued, "*his word was in mine heart as a burning fire shut up in my bones,* and I was weary with forbearing, and I could not stay" (Jeremiah 20:7, 9; emphasis added). He could not quit because of the fire of the Spirit inside him.

Ether was the last of the prophets to the Jaredite civilization. He made a comment similar to Brigham Young's and Jeremiah's. Moroni recounted Ether's efforts in crying faith and repentance from sunrise to sunset, saying, "for he could not be restrained because of the Spirit of the Lord which was in him" (Ether 12:2).

How You Can Get and Keep the Spirit

Fire is a symbol of the Holy Ghost, and of his effect on a person. How can you get the fire in your bones? How can you get the Spirit of God or the Holy Ghost inside you to make mighty changes in your life? Here is the scriptural plan, step by step, to receive such a blessing. (You may also wish to use the outline in Appendix 3 of this book to further study how to get the Spirit.)

1. *Desire it.* "Blessed are all they who do hunger and thirst after righteousness, for they shall be filled with the Holy Ghost" (3 Nephi 12:6). When you come before the throne of God hungering and thirsting (importuning!) after the things of God, you will get them. Do you really want more spirituality? You will seek it and find it. One of my valiant assistants in the mission wrote me a note one day: "President, I have never felt so close to the Spirit as I have this last week or so. I love it. I remember asking you how you knew when the Spirit was telling you what to do, or how you could always have the guidance of the Spirit. Now I know what I was missing: I never really wanted it. You've got to want it—bad! I love it! And I never want to lose it!"

2. *Be obedient; keep the commandments.* An elder sent me an observation and a question: "I try to stay worthy of the Holy Ghost and then trust that what I plan or say or do is inspired. It's tough to discern between my own thoughts and the Spirit's guidance. How can you discern between your own desires or thoughts and those that the Holy Ghost puts in

your heart and mind?" I thought about that for a while, because I faced that very issue each time I sat down before the picture-board to start making changes in missionaries' assignments. I needed immediate guidance by the Spirit and instantaneous revelation. I believe, ultimately, the answer is simple: when you are living right and truly seeking the Lord's guidance, your own thoughts become what the Spirit puts there.

I like the stories of Daniel in the Old Testament. (I would understandably be interested in someone by that name since my father's name is Daniel Howard, my own name is Daniel Kelly, and my son's name is Daniel Ben.) Some years ago, I was assigned to write the gospel doctrine lesson for the Church on the book of Daniel. It finally came to me that the real lesson from the life of Daniel wasn't the miraculous events surrounding him and his friends (the fiery furnace, the lions' den, and so forth), but the commitment to *daily diligence,* just keeping up the same righteous habits they had pursued for years. When faced with the decree not to kneel and pray to any god besides a huge idol set up by the king, or else get thrown into a den of lions, Daniel went right ahead and continued the same daily habit he had observed for eighty years: he knelt down and prayed to the true God of heaven. It

is not the "lightning and thunder" events, the miraculous and memorable moments, that ultimately make a difference in our spiritual life, but it's the struggle for daily diligence, being firm and steadfast on a daily basis, with all the little things.

3. *Learn to love and have virtuous thoughts.* Another way to have the Spirit with you always is described in Doctrine and Covenants 121:45–46. The Lord says, "Let thy bowels also be full of charity towards all men [that is all human beings], and to the household of faith [especially the Saints], and let virtue garnish thy thoughts unceasingly; then shall thy confidence wax strong in the presence of God; and . . . the Holy Ghost shall be thy constant companion."

We learn to avoid the lusts of the flesh by walking in the Spirit. One of the most talked-about events in January 1989 was the execution of the worst serial sex killer in the country's history, Ted Bundy. Eleven years after he was convicted of murdering a young Florida school girl, and after he had received several stays of execution, all the courts refused to further postpone his death date. In the final days and hours of his life he confessed to brutally killing between twenty-five and thirty women, maybe more, in five states, including one young LDS girl he kidnapped from a youth conference at BYU.

In the last interview of his life he allowed psychologist and evangelist James Dobson to interview him, and he vividly explained the motivation for his torture murders. He laid the blame squarely on pornography; he grew up ingesting lewd, aberrant stories and ideas. What was fancifully suggested to his mind, he later expanded on and acted out in all its sadistic horror. I remember listening intently to a radio broadcast of the interview in his prison cell, just hours before his life ended in the electric chair. I have never heard such a shocking warning to America to morally wake up. Bundy's mind was fed the pornography of decades ago. There are worse things channeled into everyone's living rooms nowadays, through cable and the Internet. Bundy expressed fright at what cable television was then offering to American homes. He pathetically admitted that his execution was deserved, but that his death would not resolve the nation's dilemma. Sadly, he was right. There are thousands of men like him in America right now devouring pornography that is much worse.

The scriptural solution to these conditions is simply but powerfully expressed by Paul in his letter to the Galatians:

"Walk in the Spirit, and ye shall not fulfil the lust of the flesh.

"Now the works of the flesh are manifest, which are

these; adultery, fornication, uncleanness, lasciviousness, idolatry, witchcraft, hatred, variance, emulations, wrath, strife, seditions, heresies, envyings, murders, drunkenness, revellings [and we might add today's list: masturbation, pornography, homosexual behavior, abortion, molestation, any form of sexual intimacy outside of marriage, and similar perversions], . . . [and] they which do such things shall not inherit the kingdom of God.

"But the fruit of the Spirit is love, joy, peace, longsuffering, gentleness, goodness, faith, meekness, temperance [meaning self-control]" and so on (Galatians 5:16, 19–23; emphasis added).

There are negative examples of giving in to the lusts of the flesh in the Old Testament, including Saul, David, and Solomon, for example. They murdered and transgressed morally. At some point in their lives they stopped walking in the Spirit and gave way to the lusts of the flesh. Specifically, they must have stopped studying the scriptures and praying, among other things. They were weakened, and they succumbed.

Nephi, on the other hand, is a happy example of one who continued to walk in the Spirit. He knew what to do and did it: "My soul delighteth in the scriptures, and my heart pondereth them. . . . My soul delighteth in the things of the Lord;

and my heart pondereth continually upon the things which I have seen and heard" (2 Nephi 4:15–16).

As Jesus taught, our "spirit indeed is willing, but the flesh is weak" (see Matthew 26:41). If you will walk in the Spirit by loving and serving other people and immediately expel evil thoughts and maintain clean, virtuous thoughts, you can avoid the lusts of the flesh and be filled with the Spirit of God.

4. *Fast.* This is one of the most effective ways of getting the Spirit—by temporarily setting aside the desires of your body and concentrating on what your spirit wants. Alma wrote: "I testify unto you that I do know that these things whereof I have spoken are true. And how do ye suppose that I know of their surety? Behold, I say unto you they are made known unto me by the Holy Spirit of God. Behold, I have fasted and prayed many days that I might know these things of myself. And now I do know of myself that they are true; for the Lord God hath made them manifest unto me by his Holy Spirit" (Alma 5:45–46).

5. *Pray.* Enoch was four hundred thirty years old when he was translated with his people, but many years before that "he saw the Lord, and he walked with him, and was before his face continually" (D&C 107:49). What do you think it

means when the scripture says he was "before his face continually"? Certainly one possible answer was that he prayed frequently and mightily to the Lord. He talked constantly with God; if he was not always literally talking, at least he had a prayer in his heart; therefore, the Spirit of God accompanied him. "The Spirit shall be given unto you by the prayer of faith" (D&C 42:14), the Lord promises. And he repeats the truth: "Ye receive the Spirit through prayer" (D&C 63:64).

6. *Ponder the scriptures.* The two disciples on the road to Emmaus had an impressive experience with the Spirit when the Savior taught them from the scriptures: "And they said one to another, Did not our heart burn within us, while he talked with us by the way, and while he opened to us the scriptures?" (Luke 24:32). The Spirit of God can come powerfully to your soul as you study and ponder the words of the Savior. His words are saturated with the Spirit.

7. *Remember the Savior.* Here is his assurance: "If ye do always remember me ye shall have my Spirit to be with you" (3 Nephi 18:7). And how do you remember him? By doing all of the above: keep the commandments, exercise love and virtue, fast, pray, and ponder the scriptures—and doing so with a conscious sense of gratitude to him. It is really very simple—not easy, but simple.

8. *Worship in the temple.* Have you ever heard the Lord's encouragement to "stand in holy places"? The holiest places on earth are his temples. When we are old enough and spiritually mature enough, he wants us to be worthy and then to go regularly to his holy house, at least in part because that is the place where the Spirit is strongest. The temple will help us keep our priorities straight. As important to us as the Prophet Joseph Smith and the Book of Mormon are, for example, they are not even mentioned in the temple. The temple instruction and ordinances are very focused, helping us to learn what the Father and the Son are doing with us here and how we can become like them. We make covenants to do the very things that will help us become like them. And all this happens in the most reverent and sacred attitude. The Spirit is abundant and in such a setting is able to reveal how each person can make mighty changes to become more like God.

MIGHTY RESULTS OF HAVING THE SPIRIT

1. *With the Spirit, you will have no fear.* When you have the Spirit, you don't have to be afraid of the trials and difficulties that come into your life. You have a testimony that as you are obedient your life will be in the Lord's hands and that

he will work with you according to his plan. You can be righteously bold in your behavior, like the boldness of Peter and other apostles anciently. After Jesus' Resurrection he told his Apostles to wait in Jerusalem until the Holy Ghost came upon them: "Ye shall receive power, after that the Holy Ghost is come upon you" (Acts 1:8). Then, when that great gift did come, how was their behavior different? They were changed men, and they taught with boldness (see Acts 4:8, 13). Notice what happened when the Jewish leaders prohibited them from speaking in the name of Jesus: "They called them, and commanded them not to speak at all nor teach in the name of Jesus. But Peter and John answered and said unto them, Whether it be right in the sight of God to hearken unto you more than unto God, judge ye. For we cannot but speak the things which we have seen and heard" (Acts 4:18–20). "They were all filled with the Holy Ghost, and they spake the word of God with boldness . . . and with great power" (Acts 4:31, 33). The Jewish leaders pursued the Apostles and warned them again: "Did not we straitly command you that ye should not teach in this name? and, behold, ye have filled Jerusalem with your doctrine. . . . Then Peter and the other apostles answered and said, We ought to obey God rather than men. . . . And daily in the temple, and in every house, they ceased not to teach and preach Jesus Christ" (Acts 5:28–29, 42).

When people are filled with the Spirit of God, there is no fear of what may happen to them in this mortal sphere. There is confidence that all things will ultimately work together for their good.

2. *With the Spirit, you will not be deceived.* When you treasure up the Lord's words, which are confirmed in your mind and heart by his Spirit, you will not be deceived (see Joseph Smith—Matthew 1:37). There is a lot of deception in the world, but you will not be overwhelmed or overcome by it—that is the Lord's promise.

3. *With the Spirit, you can receive forgiveness of your sins.* You can be cleansed and strengthened. Nephi wrote, "Wherefore, do the things which I have told you I have seen that your Lord and your Redeemer should do; for, for this cause have they been shown unto me, that ye might know the gate by which ye should enter. For the gate by which ye should enter is repentance and baptism by water; and then cometh a remission of your sins by fire and by the Holy Ghost" (2 Nephi 31:17).

4. *With the Spirit, you can learn all necessary things.* You can receive the revelations you need to be guided in your life.

"By the power of the Holy Ghost ye may know the truth of all things" (Moroni 10:5). "Again I say unto you that if ye will enter in by the way, and receive the Holy Ghost, it will show unto you all things what ye should do" (2 Nephi 32:5). Joseph Smith taught: "No man can receive the Holy Ghost without receiving revelations. The Holy Ghost is a revelator."[2]

5. *With the Spirit, you will be a happy person.* Regardless of trials and afflictions, you will understand how even the painful ordeals of this life are meant to teach eternally valuable lessons. You will maintain a happy outlook no matter what happens. President Heber C. Kimball, for many years a counselor to President Brigham Young, said: "I am perfectly satisfied that my Father and my God is a cheerful, pleasant, lively, and good-natured Being. Why? Because I am cheerful, pleasant, lively, and good-natured when I have His Spirit."[3]

The voice of the Spirit is a quiet voice. The scriptures call it "a still small voice" (1 Kings 19:12), "a still voice of perfect mildness" (Helaman 5:30), "a small voice" that can pierce people to the very soul, and "cause their hearts to burn" (3 Nephi 11:3). That quiet, mild, penetrating voice can be interrupted by the noises of the world. The world's noises that distract and inhibit the workings of the Spirit are sin, contention, improper videos, substance abuse, inappropriate music, and many other such things that are spiritually damaging. Even things that are otherwise appropriate—such as popular music or radio talk shows or television programs—can be distracting and can sometimes reduce our ability to receive spiritual things. Simply put, sometimes the Spirit can't get through to us because the world's noise is too loud around us. The Holy Spirit *whispers*. We need to turn the world's noise down, or turn it off, and enjoy the peace that the Holy Ghost can bring.

HOW TO RECOGNIZE THE SPIRIT

President Howard W. Hunter gave some unusual but poignant counsel: "Let me offer a word of caution on this subject [bringing the Spirit into our teaching]. I think if we are not careful . . . , we may begin to try to counterfeit the true influence of the Spirit of the Lord by unworthy and manipulative means. I get concerned when it appears that strong emotion or free-flowing tears are equated with the presence of the Spirit. Certainly the Spirit of the Lord can bring strong emotional feelings, including tears, but that outward manifestation ought not to be confused with the presence of the Spirit itself.

"I have watched a great many of my brethren over the years, and we have shared some rare and unspeakable spiritual experiences together. Those experiences have all been different, each special in its own way, and such sacred moments may or may not be accompanied by tears. Very often they are, but sometimes they are accompanied by total silence. Other times they are accompanied by joy. Always they are accompanied by a great manifestation of the truth, of revelation to the heart.

"Give [the people] gospel truth powerfully taught; that is the way to give them a spiritual experience. Let it come naturally and as it will, perhaps with the shedding of tears, but perhaps not. If what you say is the truth, and you say it purely and with honest conviction, [they] will feel the spirit of the truth being taught them and will recognize that inspiration and revelation has come into their hearts. That is how we build faith."[4]

Using Our Power Source

While living in Santiago, Chile, our electricity was often cut off for two to three hours each afternoon. Every time the power went off, our computer shut down, and our computer could have major problems when not shut down properly. To protect the computer I purchased an expensive "Blackout Buster"—a UPS (Uninterruptible Power Source). I set it up, step by step, and turned it on. A series of loud pops and foul-smelling smoke poured out of our computer. I threw open the window and abandoned the office for a time. I thought about what could have gone wrong, and finally figured it out: I had unknowingly connected a 220-volt emergency back-up battery to the rest of the computer, which is only a 110-volt system running through a large transformer. At that point I hoped I hadn't ruined all or part of our hard drive or destroyed significant parts of the operating system; I was relieved to learn I had only burned out some fuses that could be replaced.

I realized that a gospel lesson could come out of that minor catastrophe. My computer did need an Uninterruptible Power Source, and so do we. We have a marvelous power source in a gift available to every member of the Church—the gift of the Holy Ghost. But that Power Source is interruptible. Lack of prayer, scripture study, fasting, temple worship, and so on make our spiritual systems unreceptive to the power that is otherwise available. We also interfere with generating that power in us when we intentionally sin. Sin causes spiritual burnout. Without the power source of godliness—the companionship of the Holy Ghost—we are weakened and eventually become nonfunctional in a spiritual sense.

6

HOW TO BE
EXACTLY OBEDIENT

ELIZA R. SNOW WAS ONE OF THE EXCEPTIONAL writers in the latter-day Church. She was a poetess and wrote some of our best-known and best-loved hymns, such as "O My Father," "Behold the Great Redeemer Die," "Truth Reflects upon Our Senses," and "How Great the Wisdom and the Love." In verse three of "How Great the Wisdom and the Love," Sister Snow wrote, "By strict obedience Jesus won the prize with glory rife."[1] Even Jesus, the greatest person ever to live on this earth, won the prize of eternal glory only by strict obedience to the will of his Father.

When I returned from the Holy Land and began working with the elders and sisters in the Missionary Training Center, I was impressed with how often the missionaries were encouraged in talks, handbooks, bulletins, and memos to be "exactly" obedient and "strictly" obedient. Yes, the first law of heaven is obedience,[2] but it was vital that those going out to represent the Lord Jesus Christ be *exactly* obedient and *strictly* obedient. Unfortunately, I don't think those two words are very popular in the world these days. Young people demand freedom; they don't want to be restricted by mountains of rules. Yet hundreds of thousands of missionaries over the decades have been taught to be exactly and strictly obedient, in all things.

I also recall the first few times I attended the holy temple, just before going on my first mission. I was a little surprised when, in the middle of a session, the officiator sometimes stopped the entire group to fix something that wasn't positioned just right or that wasn't done correctly. I thought, "My, this is rather meticulous—everything has to be done in exactly the right way." I soon learned that meticulous order was indeed expected; all things needed to be in their proper place—for the Lord was teaching us that his house is a house of order. He was teaching us to get prepared to live in the most refined society in the heavens—to learn exact obedience to the God of heaven, because that is the only way we will become like him.

EXAMPLES OF EXACT OBEDIENCE

We have a host of examples preserved in sacred records of those who have demonstrated their willingness to obey all things the Lord commands. Take the first man, for instance. We read in the book of Moses that the Lord gave commandments to Adam and Eve "that they should worship the Lord their God, and should offer the firstlings of their flocks, for an offering unto the Lord. And Adam was obedient unto the commandments of the Lord" (Moses 5:5).

That obedience continued for "many days." Then, after the passage of time, "an angel of the Lord appeared unto Adam, saying: Why dost thou offer sacrifices unto the Lord? And Adam said unto him: I know not, save the Lord commanded me" (Moses 5:6).

Even though he had no idea why he was doing it, Adam sought to do exactly what the Lord asked of him. Of course, the Lord ultimately wanted Adam to understand the sacred symbolism involved in offering blood sacrifices, and he sent his angel to explain the meaning of the ordinance to Adam. But first he tested Adam's obedience, to see if he was willing to do precisely what the Lord asked—even without knowing the reasons.

Some people might object to that, calling that kind of scrupulous submissiveness "blind obedience." Elder Spencer W. Kimball responded to that objection by saying, "Blind obedience? Assuredly not. They had known Jehovah, heard his voice, walked with him in the Garden of Eden, and knew of his goodness, justice, and understanding. And so for 'many days' they killed the blemishless lambs and offered them without knowing why, but in total confidence that there was righteous purpose in the law and that the reason would unfold later after compliance."[3]

The obedience of our first parents to the specific instructions of the Lord is an example of what the mortal Jesus later taught: "If any man will do [the Father's] will, he shall know of the doctrine" (John 7:17). Doing exactly what the Lord asks will result in our comprehending the doctrines of eternity and realizing their ultimate benefit to us.

Elder Kimball taught: "Often we hear: 'Nobody can tell me what clothes to wear, what I shall eat or drink. No one can outline my Sabbaths, appropriate my earnings, nor in any way limit my personal freedoms! I do as I please! I give no *blind obedience!* . . . When men obey commands of a creator, it is not blind obedience. How different is the cowering of a subject to his totalitarian monarch and the dignified, willing obedience one gives to his God. The dictator is ambitious, selfish, and has ulterior motives. God's every command is righteous, every directive purposeful, and all for the good of the governed. The first may be blind obedience, but the latter is certainly faith obedience."[4]

Adam and Eve strictly obeyed the commands of God and received the corresponding blessings. From the beginning, they provided a happy example to their posterity.

Noah was another superb example. Long before the rains came, while it was still dry, the Lord commanded him to build a ship to save his family from a great flood. That would be like the Lord commanding his servant, Brother Ogden, to take his family from Provo, Utah, and flee up the canyon eastward into Heber Valley, and there build a spaceship. The world would soon be destroyed, and that would be the only way for my family and me to escape and be saved. My reaction, of course, would be "But Lord, I don't know how to build a spaceship." I suspect Noah must have felt the same way. But he responded. He did exactly as the Lord instructed him (the Lord providing the details after Noah demonstrated his willingness to obey), and, in the end, the prophet and his family were saved and thus perpetuated the human race. We all appreciate Noah's obedience: we are all descendants of

Noah, and his obedience preserved our option to come here for this crucial mortal probation.

Abraham and Sarah are classic examples of faith and obedience. Elder Bruce R. McConkie wrote: "I would suppose that among faithful people in ancient Israel, through all the ages from Abraham's day onward, the favored illustration and the favored text to teach the people that the Only Begotten Son would be sacrificed to bring immortality to men would be the story of Abraham. There is nothing more dramatic than this in the whole biblical account."[5]

Abraham and Sarah were already old, with Sarah past age to have a child of her own, when the word of the Lord came to them, saying they would have a son. And what did Sarah do? She laughed. The Hebrew verb used in Genesis does mean to laugh, but it also means to rejoice—and I don't doubt she did both. She must have smiled at the idea of giving birth in her advanced age, but at the same time she knew the Lord and trusted him; if he said she would have a son, she would have a son. That son was born, and they loved him.

Then came the supreme trial of their faith and obedience. We will follow the dramatic story as recorded in Genesis 22. Verse 1 says that God tempted Abraham. The word *tempt* means to test, try, or prove. Here indeed was a test for

Abraham: "Take now thy son, thine only son Isaac, whom thou lovest . . . " (verse 2). Was Isaac his only son? No, he had another son, Ishmael, from Hagar (his second wife), but the wording is very particular. This was the only son from his first wife; this was the promised son; and he was the beloved son. Paul later wrote that "by faith Abraham, when he was tried, offered up Isaac: and he that had received the promises offered up his *only begotten son*" (Hebrews 11:17; emphasis added).

The command came to offer that beloved son as a burnt offering on a mount called Moriah (later to be known as Jerusalem's Temple Mount). Abraham knew how repulsive human sacrifice was and how foreign such a practice is to the true worship of our Heavenly Father. He himself, as a youth, had nearly been sacrificed on an idolatrous altar by apostate priests, and it took an angel from heaven to rescue him and preserve his life. (See Abraham 1:5–20 and Abraham facsimile 1.) But Abraham knew something else, too. He knew that one of God's expressed purposes for his children during mortality was to "prove them herewith, to see if they will do *all things* whatsoever the Lord their God shall command them" (Abraham 3:25; emphasis added). God had commanded it; how could he not obey?

Some years ago a group of BYU Jerusalem Study Abroad students and I began a three-day journey in the footsteps of Abraham and Isaac—from Beersheba to Mount Moriah in Jerusalem. That first morning as we rode the bus to Beersheba to begin the fifty-three-mile walk, we asked ourselves, "Why did the Lord send Abraham (who was well over a hundred years old by this time) more than fifty miles away, and *uphill;* why not send him to one of the nearby hills in the Negev Desert, where he lived? What was so special about Mount Moriah to the Lord or to Abraham?" The more we thought about it, the more likely it seemed that Moriah was already a significant sacred spot in the days of Abraham. Maybe Melchizedek had a holy temple at Salem, where the mount stood. Perhaps Abraham already knew that Moriah in future centuries would be a place of many temple sacrifices, all in anticipation of the Great Sacrifice which would be accomplished there. He certainly knew something about the great atoning drama that would unfold there in the meridian of time.

The Book of Mormon prophet Jacob taught that Abraham's poignant trial, the offering up of his son Isaac, was "a similitude of God and his Only Begotten Son" (Jacob 4:5). Abraham and Isaac not only experienced the same kind of ordeal, feeling similar deep and agonizing feelings, but they accomplished it at the same place where the Father would later sacrifice his Beloved Son. Abraham was called on to sacrifice, to *give up,* the best he had, as our Heavenly Father would give the best he had.

Abraham and Isaac walked along for three days, plenty of time to think about what was coming. Isaac then asked the heart-rending question, "My father, . . . behold the fire and the wood: but where is the lamb for a burnt offering?" (Genesis 22:7). Abraham prophetically responded, "My son, God will provide himself a lamb for a burnt offering" (Genesis 22:8). The term for God in the Hebrew text of this verse is *Elohim.* An *olah* is a whole burnt offering, literally, "that which goes up to heaven from the altar." The offering had to be a perfect male. A male lamb without blemish was offered by individuals and the nation as atonement for sins, and according to Leviticus 1:11, when a lamb was slain on the great altar of the temple it was slain on the north side of the altar (Golgotha, the place of Jesus' execution, was on the north side of Moriah).

When Abraham's test was passed and the angel of the Lord was sent to stop the sacrifice of the son, a ram (not a *lamb*) was substituted. (Note: The prophecy of a *lamb,* even the *Lamb of God*, which was known from the foundation of the world, would yet be fulfilled.) Then "Abraham called the name of that place Jehovah-jireh: as it is said to this day, In the mount of the Lord it shall be seen" (Genesis 22:14). In the final phrase of verse 14, the English words *of* and *it* do not appear in the original; the phrase should read, "In the mount [and many manuscripts read 'In *this* mount,' meaning Moriah] the Lord shall be seen, or, the Lord shall be provided." As in verse 8, when Abraham promised that Elohim (the Father) would provide a lamb for the sacrifice, in verse 14 Abraham notes that Jehovah (the Son) will appear—he will be seen or "provided" on the mount.

All of this seems to signify that Abraham knew something of the meaning of his similitude-sacrifice. He had uttered prophetically—and seemingly with deeper understanding—that our Heavenly Father would provide a lamb as a sacrifice or atonement for sin, and he knew that the Son would be that sacrifice, to be made at that very place. Said Jesus, centuries later at that same place, "Your father Abraham rejoiced to see my day: and he saw it, and was glad" (John 8:56).

Abraham, our ancestor, is our model. "Abraham received all things, whatsoever he received, by revelation and commandment, by my word, saith the Lord, and hath entered into his exaltation and sitteth upon his throne. . . . Go ye, therefore, and do the works of Abraham. . . .

"Abraham was commanded to offer his son Isaac; nevertheless, it was written: Thou shalt not kill. Abraham, however, did not refuse, and it was accounted unto him for righteousness. . . . He abode in my law; as Isaac also and Jacob did none other things than that which they were commanded; and because they did none other things than that which they were commanded, they have entered into their exaltation" (D&C 132:29, 32, 36, 37).

"They did none other things than that which they were commanded"—as with the Savior, by strict obedience Abraham also won the prize of eternal life. The Lord could make great promises to Abraham, even before the tests and trials, for he said of his servant Abraham: "I know him, that he will command his children and his household after him, and they shall keep the way of the Lord, . . . that the Lord may bring upon Abraham that which he hath spoken of him" (Genesis 18:19).

What a remarkable commentary God made about the faithfulness of our ancestor. Can he make a similar statement about you? Does he know you so well that he can pronounce great blessings upon you, as in your patriarchal blessing, and rest assured that you will be obedient—so that you will definitely fulfill those blessings?

Joseph Smith declared, "Whatever God requires is right."[6] Following Abraham's example we will obey, no matter what the command, for we know that God gives no commandments to us without preparing the way for us to accomplish them (recall the testimony of Nephi, as recorded in 1 Nephi 3:7).

Lehi was willing to leave his homeland of Jerusalem without a lot of explanation. The Lord told him to pack up and abandon the city, not expecting to ever return. Many Saints through the ages, especially full-time missionaries, have left their homes to serve the Lord (though they expected to return). It is not easy to leave our home, but God calls and we obey.

Nephi was instructed to make two sets of plates without knowing why. That was a big order; as the Book of Mormon writers remind us, it was hard work making metal plates and hard work engraving them. Nephi explained: "The Lord hath commanded me to make these plates for a wise purpose in him, which purpose I know not. But the Lord knoweth all things from the beginning; wherefore, he prepareth a way to accomplish all his works among the children of men" (1 Nephi 9:5–6). We have the advantage of knowing that in the early nineteenth century Martin Harris would take the first manuscript pages of the one record and lose them, something the Lord clearly foresaw. The Lord had a contingency plan in mind for thousands of years: the parallel set of plates was then called in to substitute wonderfully for that which was lost. We don't know that Nephi ever learned the reason why he had to go to all that extra work, but he was willing to be expressly obedient to what the Lord, in his wisdom, directed his prophet to do.

Such are some of the marvelous examples we find in our scriptures of how to be exactly obedient. Often the Lord tells us why we are to obey a commandment, but sometimes he doesn't—but we learn to trust him and carry out his will even if we don't understand why. Sometimes, as Robert Frost wrote (see chapter three), it is the essence of the trial that we should not understand it at the time.

Among modern missionaries there are also brilliant examples of how to obey. One missionary wrote to me: "I came to Chile to baptize, not to be obedient. Now I obey so I can baptize. All my life I have been obedient, but not with exactness. If I accomplish only one thing in my mission, I want to learn to be exactly obedient. I've always been obedient just to please my parents; now I want to be obedient for my Heavenly Father and for Jesus Christ."

Before returning home, our missionaries prepared two lists: what they learned from the mission experience, and what they came to appreciate. One elder wrote: "I learned a lot here in the mission. Now I know how to obey. If a missionary goes back home without learning this principle, he didn't learn much. In the mission we have many rules, but I came to realize that when I was obeying and really trying to live every rule that God was going to bless me. We had success because my companion and I were keeping all the rules."

Another elder wrote: "When I was serving in the armed forces I learned obedience and discipline because of love for my country. Now I've learned obedience and discipline because of my love of God and his Son, Jesus Christ. Actually, the first discipline was forced on us and was easier to achieve, but in the mission there is a self-discipline that is more difficult because we try to make excuses and rationalize—but it is at this point that we truly show our sincere love. The more obedient we are, the more valiant we are."

WHY WE WANT TO OBEY

Can we obey all the "big" commandments and disregard the little ones? Of course not. Can we obey all the "little" commandments and disregard the big ones? No, that would be like the Pharisees, wouldn't it? Jesus made it clear that he hates hypocrisy: "Woe unto you, scribes and Pharisees, hypocrites! for ye pay tithe of mint and anise and cummin, and have omitted the weightier matters of the law, judgment, mercy, and faith: these ought ye to have done, and not to leave the other undone" (Matthew 23:23). Our God expects us to obey all things—big and little.

Brigham Young said: "Truth is obeyed when it is loved. Strict obedience to the truth will alone enable people to dwell in the presence of the Almighty."[7]

There is a crucial principle all of us must learn of *yielding,* being *submissive* to the will of the Lord—and doing so out of love for the Eternal Father and his eternal truths. Look at the well-known verse, Mosiah 3:19, and you will clearly see this crucial principle. The concept appears four times in this single verse:

"For the natural man is an enemy to God, and has been from the fall of Adam, and will be, forever and ever, unless he *yields* to the enticings of the Holy Spirit, and putteth off the natural man and becometh a saint through the atonement of Christ the Lord, and becometh as a child, *submissive,* meek, humble, patient, full of love, willing to *submit* to all things which the Lord seeth fit to inflict upon him, even as a child doth *submit* to his father" (emphasis added).

The terms *yield* and *submit* and *submissive*—which appear more than any other words in the verse—are essential keys to our putting off the natural man and becoming a true Saint.

Later in the Book of Mormon, a few decades before the Savior's visit to the Nephite people, we have a passage that describes how a group of people became sanctified—how they became true Saints:

"They did fast and pray oft, and did wax stronger and stronger in their humility, and firmer and firmer in the faith of Christ, unto the filling their souls with joy and consolation, yea, even to the purifying and the sanctification of their hearts, which sanctification cometh because of their *yielding* their hearts unto God" (Helaman 3:35; emphasis added). There it is again. People were purified because they *yielded their hearts to God.* They desired to be strictly obedient in all things. They were humble and teachable, willing to listen and obey even all the "little rules."

Verse 3 of Sister Eliza Snow's hymn reminds us that "'thy will, O God, not mine be done,' adorned his mortal life."[8] It is a matter of daily diligence, isn't it? It is a habit of daily discipline.

One warning: We get in trouble when we think we are an

exception to a rule, when we feel we are above some commandment. That is what happened with each one of Israel's first three kings: Saul, David, and Solomon. All three of those kings were spiritual men, close to the Lord in their early lives. Then they started slipping in the most important habits of obedience. We not only have to desire exact obedience, but we have to work hard to achieve it; then we have to watch ourselves carefully to maintain that level of faithfulness. Keys to faithfulness include careful attendance to four things: prayer, scripture study, temple worship, and serving others. We will stay true and faithful, obeying the Lord in all things, if we will continue, without fail, in those four habits of obedience.

7

HOW TO GET RID
OF PRIDE

YEARS AGO I SAW A MOVIE CALLED *Wild Hearts Can't Be Broken*. The movie was good, but it was the title that held me captive for quite some time. I kept thinking about the words of that title. Maybe some think it's true that wild hearts can't be broken—but is that good gospel doctrine?

What does the Lord want of us? "I, the Lord, require the hearts of the children of men" (D&C 64:22). And in what condition does he want our hearts? "Come unto me with a *broken* heart" (3 Nephi 12:19; emphasis added; see also D&C 56:18; 97:8).

What does the Lord mean by a broken heart? Of course he is not referring to the little one-pound pump inside our breasts, which pumps blood through the sixty thousand miles of blood vessels in our bodies once a minute throughout our entire mortal lives. He is certainly not suggesting it would be good to have that extraordinary instrument broken. Nor do I believe he is referring to how we feel when we say we are "broken-hearted," meaning we are devastated because of a broken relationship with another person.

In ancient and modern scripture the heart is the symbolic center of our deepest and most vital emotions. The Savior wants our feelings to be humble, to be contrite (the word *contrite* comes from a Latin term meaning "bruised"; we are wounded or humbled and penitent—spiritually bruised—because of our weaknesses and natural sinfulness). If we are truly contrite about our native, telestial inclination to sin, we will feel dependent on God and humbly seek him. On the other hand, if we are delighting in our sinfulness, the lusts of the flesh, and the accumulation of the things of the world, we are probably feeling too independent; we feel we don't need God and are caught up in pride; we are feeling self-sufficient and proud of what we ourselves have achieved. (Note: In the scriptures there is no such thing as righteous pride. In this chapter we are talking about the sin of pride.)

The renowned Christian philosopher and writer, C. S. Lewis, gave one of the most brilliant descriptions of pride ever penned. While you read his words, look for how he defines it, how he labels its destructive nature, and how it manifests itself:

"There is one vice of which no man in the world is free; which every one in the world loathes when he sees it in someone else; and of which hardly any people . . . ever imagine that they are guilty themselves. I have heard people admit that they are bad-tempered, or that they cannot keep their heads about girls or drink, or even that they are cowards. I do not think I have ever heard anyone . . . accuse himself of this vice. And at the same time I have very seldom met anyone . . . who showed the slightest mercy to it in others. There is no fault which makes a man more unpopular, and no fault which we are more unconscious of in ourselves. And the more we have it ourselves, the more we dislike it in others.

"The vice I am talking of is Pride or Self-Conceit: and the virtue opposite to it . . . is called Humility. You may remember, when I was talking about sexual morality, I warned you that the centre of Christian morals did not lie there. Well, now, we have come to the centre. According to Christian teachers, the essential vice, the utmost evil, is Pride. Unchastity, anger, greed, drunkenness, and all that, are mere fleabites in comparison: it was through Pride that the devil became the devil: Pride leads to every other vice: it is the complete anti-God state of mind.

"Does this seem to you exaggerated? If so, think it over. I pointed out a moment ago that the more pride one had, the more one disliked pride in others. In fact, if you want to find out how proud you are the easiest way is to ask yourself, 'How much do I dislike it when other people snub me, or refuse to take any notice of me . . . or patronise me, or show off?' The point is that each person's pride is in competition with every one else's pride. It is because I wanted to be the big noise at the party that I am so annoyed at someone else being the big noise. Two of a trade never agree. Now what you want to get clear is that Pride is *essentially* competitive—is competitive by its very nature—while the other vices are competitive only, so to speak, by accident. Pride gets no pleasure out of having something, only out of having more of it than the next man. We say that people are proud of being rich, or clever, or good-looking, but they are not. They are proud of being richer, or cleverer, or better-looking than others. If everyone else became equally rich, or clever, or good-looking there would be nothing to be proud about. It is the comparison that makes you proud: the pleasure of being above the rest. Once the element of competition has gone, pride has gone.

. . . Nearly all those evils in the world which people put down to greed or selfishness are really far more the result of Pride."[1]

KEY SCRIPTURAL TEACHINGS ABOUT PRIDE

"The day cometh," the Lord says, "that shall burn as an oven; and all the proud, yea, and all that do wickedly, shall be stubble" (Malachi 4:1). Notice that while warning of the time of judgment that is imminent, the Lord singles out one sin, pride. All other sinning he lumps together in "all that do wickedly." There apparently is one sin that God hates above all, for he knows how pride obstructs our opportunity to learn of him and desire to become like him. Pride is "my will" instead of "thy will." One of the reasons we have all come to this earth life, this "probation location," is to eradicate a rebellion complex we all have, an inclination to do things our own way, and learn to submit to His way—the only way salvation can ever come to us.

"For," as King Benjamin reminds us, "the natural man is an enemy to God, and has been from the fall of Adam, and will be, forever and ever, unless he yields to the enticings of the Holy Spirit, and putteth off the natural man and becometh a saint through the atonement of Christ the Lord, and becometh as a child, submissive, meek, humble, patient, full of love, willing to submit to all things which the Lord seeth fit to inflict upon him, even as a child doth submit to his father" (Mosiah 3:19).

There are certain key verbs and adjectives in that verse that are crucial to our eradicating the rebellion complex we suffer from. The verbs are *yield* and *submit.* The adjectives are *submissive, meek, humble, patient,* and *willing.* Our God expects us to learn of him and submit to his will. That is the basic concept of Islam, which word itself means *submission.* A true Muslim is one who submits to the will of *Allah* (Arabic "God," parallel to the Hebrew *Elohim*). The doctrine of submitting ourselves to God's will, and not pursuing our own will, is true doctrine, as King Benjamin testified.

The first verses of John 15 contain one of the most beautiful and powerful analogies in all the world's literature. There Jesus taught that we gain strength and nourishment from the true Vine. Only the branch that stays firmly connected to the Vine and its roots can drink deeply of the Water of Life and absorb the Sun of Righteousness and all other necessary nutrients to assure growth leading to fruitfulness. Despite the prunings (the trials of life), when the branch is cut down (humbled)—or actually *because of* such prunings—the branch can be made more fruitful. Those who remain unproductive in the end will be cut off and burned in the fire.

"Abide in me, . . . abide in the vine" (John 15:4), Jesus said, meaning that we must remain connected, persist, endure, continue, persevere. All of these action verbs suggest our need to stay close to the Savior. We are totally dependent on him, as sheep are dependent on their shepherd.

Some years ago I took my children a number of times to help a woman operate a petting farm for children in Mapleton, Utah. One day the owner told me that if she ever had to get rid of her animals, she would keep her horses and her sheep. I could see why the horses, but I asked her why she would want to keep the dirty, smelly, noisy sheep. She said something I will never forget: "Sheep have a willingness to be dependent."

It took me a while to realize the profound significance of her remark. And I learned why the Good Shepherd has often referred to us as his sheep. He wants us to be dependent upon him. Although there is something to say about the virtue of exercising our independence and agency to do a lot of good, of our own free will (since the power to do so is in us; see D&C 58:27–28), yet in another sense we must be dependent on him—for we have, in the end, absolutely no power whatever to save ourselves. We need his grace and his merits, his atoning sacrifice, to change our present fallen condition to something more heavenly. We will never make it without him. Actually, we *cannot* change without him.

So it is with this image of the Vine. The only way we will be productive or fruitful is to stay attached to our source of strength and nourishment. "For without me," Jesus warned, "ye can do nothing" (John 15:5). Whether back then as a fisherman, a publican, or a political zealot, or today as a teacher, a government worker, or a computer consultant, in the end we will all be undistinguished nobodies if we fail to abide in him. We will produce nothing of real, lasting value.

Without him we really will amount to nothing. An old Chinese proverb says, "Man wrapped up in self make mighty small package." There is no room for God in a man who is full of himself.

Jesus taught, "Blessed are the poor in spirit" (Matthew 5:3)—that is, the "poor in pride, humble in spirit" (footnote 5:3b). The Nephite record makes a significant addition: "Blessed are the poor in spirit *who come unto me*" (3 Nephi 12:3). We must be willing to be dependent on our Savior. We are specifically told to remember our own nothingness (see Mosiah 4:11). The nothingness we refer to here is our incapacity and helplessness to get ourselves out of this fallen, mortal condition. We are not suggesting that we are worthless (nothingness is not worthlessness), because we know each soul is worth a great deal in the sight of God. The recognition of our nothingness should not lead us to hopelessness, but to willing dependence on the only Person in the universe who can rescue us from our fallen condition. The opposite of dependence is pride, which always drives us away from God (when we feel independent, we think we don't need God). Doctrine and Covenants 56:18 adds: "Blessed are the poor who are pure in heart, whose hearts are broken, and whose spirits are contrite, for they shall see the kingdom of God coming in power and great glory unto their deliverance."

There are pointed warnings given in the scriptures to avoid the dangerous trap of pride. Speaking through Brigham Young, the Lord counseled the Camp of Israel as they moved westward across the plains: "If any man shall seek to build up himself, and seeketh not my counsel, he shall have no power, and his folly shall be made manifest" (D&C 136:19). There is the warning: Don't try to build up yourself, but build up God in the eyes of the people. Do things with an eye single to the glory of God—not with an "I" single to the glory of God.

When you learn to do that here on earth, you will find yourself crowned with glory in the next world—glory unimaginable.

Joseph Smith warned that we must "not seek to excel one above another."[2] At first glance you might think, "Well, I thought we were supposed to be in the pursuit of excellence. Don't we believe in excelling?" Yes, of course we believe in doing all that we do in the most excellent way possible, but the Prophet's point was that we should not be trying to excel *one above another.* In this life we are not in competition with each other (that is one of those basic elements of pride). There is always danger in comparing ourselves with others. Comparison is the root of all feelings of inferiority. There will always be someone better than you, always someone more accomplished—even in your best abilities. Rather than striving for superiority and feeling satisfaction when you have surpassed another person, seek a personal best. Keep surpassing your own previous best, always remembering what Jesus said: "Without me ye can do nothing" (John 15:5).

RESISTING THE SPIRIT OF PRIDE

Don't blame your problems on others. "Personality conflict" is probably a concept we invented to make ourselves feel better about a relationship with someone else that isn't going well. When feeble efforts at repentance, understanding, and reconciliation fail, we throw up our arms in exasperation and give up, labeling the problem with the remark, "Oh, he and I just have a personality conflict." But what is the real problem? It is pride—usually in both individuals. It takes two to contend.

Even if the other person really is more responsible for the problem than you are, what should you do? The gospel teaches that you should humble yourself, go to the other person, and apologize for your role in the conflict (see Matthew 5:24; 18:15). When you have the Spirit with you, you will want to humble yourself and resolve all friction between you and any other person—because you want the Spirit of God in your life and because relationships matter. Talk things out with them. And be sincere about it, or the reconciliation will go nowhere.

If you are filled with too much pride, you will not want to take the initial steps, to be the first to say that you are sorry and that you seek forgiveness. But, oh, how healing it is to have a broken heart, to humble yourself and desire to make all things right with all people. When you do proceed in that manner, the Spirit will flood into your life.

Avoid contending or arguing. Arguing—whether it is emotionally charged, half-suppressed threatenings that barely

escape the lips, or loud and vicious bellowings that rever-
berate through the whole house—is motivated by the adversary. "By pride cometh contention" (Proverbs 13:10). The
necessity of defending one's position at all costs, even to the
physical or emotional injury of another person, can never be
attributed to righteous motives. The spirit of contention truly
is of the devil (3 Nephi 11:29). We must root it out. As I
always instructed my children while pulling weeds in the garden and flower beds: "Don't just pull off the top of the weed.
You have to get it out by the roots, or we'll be right back here
next week pulling out the same weed."

How do we root out contention? Admit it is a problem.
Pray more. Study the Savior's words on the matter. Fast more.
Do whatever is necessary to get rid of the underlying pride.
Seek forgiveness—and then see how much better you feel
inside.

Avoid fault-finding. It is easy to find fault with someone
else. We all have faults, and plenty of them. Work on *overcoming* your own faults and *overlooking* the faults of others.
"Thou shalt not speak evil of thy neighbor" (D&C 42:27).
Ben Franklin and other great souls (great even though they
readily recognized their own flaws) adopted a practice that
could greatly enlarge all of our souls. Here is a new adage to

live by: "I will speak ill of no person, and I will speak all the good I can of every person."

Avoid criticizing. Seldom does criticizing another person help to resolve anything. It normally deepens wounds and ruins relationships. We have created a phrase to help us feel better about our destructive efforts—we call it "constructive criticism." "Oh, it's just meant to help that other person," you think. But if you know that any part of what you are saying could be damaging, it is better left unsaid. There are ways to make suggestions for improvement, of course, but if words could be misconstrued and seen as a personal attack on another, it may be better to say only positive things and allow that person to discover and resolve the problem for himself.

Joseph Smith said, "If you have evil feelings, and speak of them to one another, it has a tendency to do mischief. . . . I would to God that you would be wise. I now counsel you, that if you know anything calculated to disturb the peace or injure the feelings of your brother or sister, hold your tongues and the least harm will be done."[3]

He also observed, "The nearer we get to our heavenly Father, the more we are disposed to look with compassion on perishing souls; we feel that we want to take them upon our shoulders, and cast their sins behind our backs."[4]

Avoid feeling you are indispensable (because you are not).
The Apostle Paul advised every man "not to think of himself more highly than he ought to think" (Romans 12:3). To realize that God's work has gone forward for ages past, or will continue on for eternities to come—with or without *me*—is to come to grips with the truth, and it is humbling. You and I would do well to be humbly grateful for whatever little temporary part we can play in the Father's great eternal plan for this earth. There is no room for pride in that attitude.

President Wilford Woodruff cautioned: "We have no chance to be lifted up in the pride of our hearts with regard to the position we occupy. If the President of the Church or either of his counselors or [if] the apostles or any other man feels in his heart that God cannot do without him, and that he is especially important in order to carry on the work of the Lord, he stands upon slippery ground. I heard Joseph Smith say that Oliver Cowdery, who was the second apostle in this Church, said to him, 'If I leave this Church it will fall.'

"Said Joseph, 'Oliver, you try it.' Oliver tried it. He fell; but the kingdom of God did not. I have been acquainted with other apostles in my day and time who felt that the Lord could not do without them; but the Lord got along with his work without them. I say to all men—Jew and Gentile, great and small, rich and poor—that the Lord Almighty has power within himself, and is not dependent upon any man, to carry on his work; but when he does call men to do his work they have to trust in him."[5]

BEWARE OF PRIDE

One of the best discussions on pride—and why we must eliminate it from our lives, comes from a great latter-day prophet, Ezra Taft Benson. Here are some excerpts from his address on this subject:

"When pride has a hold on our hearts, we lose our independence of the world and deliver our freedoms to the bondage of men's judgment. The world shouts louder than the whisperings of the Holy Ghost. The reasoning of men overrides the revelations of God, and the proud let go of the iron rod. (See 1 Ne. 8:19–28; 11:25; 15:23–24.)

"Pride is a sin that can readily be seen in others but is rarely admitted in ourselves. Most of us consider pride to be a sin of those on the top, such as the rich and the learned, looking down at the rest of us. (See 2 Ne. 9:42.) There is, however, a far more common ailment among us—and that is pride from the bottom looking up. It is manifest in so many ways, such as faultfinding, gossiping, backbiting, murmuring, living beyond our means, envying, coveting, withholding gratitude and praise that might lift another, and being unforgiving and jealous.

"Disobedience is essentially a prideful power struggle against someone in authority over us. It can be a parent, a priesthood leader, a teacher, or ultimately God. A proud person hates the fact that someone is above him. He thinks this lowers his position.

"Selfishness is one of the more common faces of pride. 'How everything affects me' is the center of all that matters—self-conceit, self-pity, worldly self-fulfillment, self-gratification, and self-seeking. . . .

"Another face of pride is contention. Arguments, fights, unrighteous dominion, generation gaps, divorces, spouse abuse, riots, and disturbances all fall into this category of pride.

"Contention in our families drives the Spirit of the Lord away. It also drives many of our family members away. Contention ranges from a hostile spoken word to worldwide conflicts. . . .

"The scriptures testify that the proud are easily offended and hold grudges. (See 1 Ne. 16:1–3.) They withhold forgiveness to keep another in their debt and to justify their injured feelings.

"The proud do not receive counsel or correction easily. (See Prov. 15:10; Amos 5:10.) Defensiveness is used by them to justify and rationalize their frailties and failures. (See Matt. 3:9; John 6:30–59.)

"The proud depend upon the world to tell them whether they have value or not. Their self-esteem is determined by where they are judged to be on the ladders of worldly success. They feel worthwhile as individuals if the numbers beneath them in achievement, talent, beauty, or intellect are large enough. Pride is ugly. It says, 'If you succeed, I am a failure.'

"If we love God, do His will, and fear His judgment more than men's, we will have self-esteem.

"Pride is a damning sin in the true sense of that word. It limits or stops progression. (See Alma 12:10–11.) The proud are not easily taught. (See 1 Ne. 15:3, 7–11.) They won't change their minds to accept truths, because to do so implies they have been wrong.

"Pride adversely affects all our relationships—our relationship with God and His servants, between husband and wife, parent and child, employer and employee, teacher and student, and all mankind. Our degree of pride determines how we treat our God and our brothers and sisters. Christ wants to lift us to where He is. Do we desire to do the same for others?

"Pride fades our feelings of sonship to God and brotherhood to man. It separates and divides us by 'ranks,' according to our 'riches' and our 'chances for learning.' (3 Ne. 6:12.) Unity is impossible for a proud people, and unless we are one we are not the Lord's. (See Mosiah 18:21; D&C 38:27; 105:2–4; Moses 7:18.) . . .

"God will have a humble people. Either we can choose to be humble or we can be compelled to be humble. Alma said, 'Blessed are they who humble themselves without being compelled to be humble.' (Alma 32:16.)

"Let us choose to be humble.

"We can choose to humble ourselves by conquering enmity toward our brothers and sisters, esteeming them as ourselves, and lifting them as high or higher than we are. (See D&C 38:24; 81:5; 84:106.)

"We can choose to humble ourselves by receiving counsel and chastisement. (See Jacob 4:10; Hel. 15:3; D&C 63:55; 101:4–5; 108:1; 124:61, 84; 136:31; Prov. 9:8.)

"We can choose to humble ourselves by forgiving those who have offended us. (See 3 Ne. 13:11, 14; D&C 64:10.)

"We can choose to humble ourselves by rendering selfless service. (See Mosiah 2:16–17.)

"We can choose to humble ourselves by going on missions and preaching the word that can humble others. (See Alma 4:19; 31:5; 48:20.)

"We can choose to humble ourselves by getting to the temple more frequently.

"We can choose to humble ourselves by confessing and forsaking our sins and being born of God. (See D&C 58:43; Mosiah 27:25–26; Alma 5:7–14, 49.)

"We can choose to humble ourselves by loving God, submitting our will to His, and putting Him first in our lives."[6]

8

HOW TO OBTAIN THE LOVE OF CHRIST

I KNOW THAT FAITH IS THE FIRST principle of the gospel. Repentance is the number one doctrine of the kingdom. Obedience is the first law of heaven. And happiness is the object of our existence. But of all things in the gospel, in the scriptures, and in the plan of salvation, that which is *most important* of all is the *love of God.*

Circumstances and people come into our lives to teach us important lessons. My wife, Marcia, has written: "Anger, irritation, annoyance, all from below. My, how the devil loves to separate people: spouses from each other, children from parents, ward members from each other, brothers and sisters, etc. Catherine Thomas said that the reason we have abrasive people in our lives is so we can learn to develop divine love.

This life is a laboratory for practicing divine love. And until we get the hang of it, we will have one irritating person after another come into our lives to give us plenty of practice."[1]

Here is an example: A woman came into my mission office in Santiago, Chile, requesting a moment to speak with me. It turned out to be more like a half-hour, and it was terribly exasperating. She wanted to talk to someone about getting her name removed from the membership records of this "incorrect" church. "I've learned," she announced, "that this is not the true way back to God, and I want to go back to my other church and just live by my Bible. I don't believe that the Book of Mormon is God's word, and I don't believe Joseph Smith was a prophet. I don't want anything to do with this church anymore." And so she carried on and on. I felt irritation mounting in me, and I tried to insert some counter-arguments here and there, especially some testimony, but it all fell on deaf ears. She was most sincere, but her heart was closed.

Near the end of her tirade, a specific thought came to my mind: "What would Jesus do in this situation?" That calmed me down, and I began feeling pain and compassion for her. She had accused us all with these words: "Your missionaries only want to baptize people, and then they leave them and don't care for them." It came to me as clearly as if I had just defrosted the windshield of my soul: Her problem was that no one had shown her the love she needed. She just needed some honest-to-goodness *love*. She may have been hard for others to love, but she needed it anyway.

I have learned about the love of God from various people in my life: family, missionary companions, my eternal companion, our children, students, colleagues, and the missionaries. In addition, I have learned a great deal by studying and pondering the words of the Savior.

Here is a summary of what love is, why we want it, how we get it, the blessings that come from having it, and its visible influence in our lives. If you will ponder carefully and prayerfully what the Lord teaches in the following paragraphs, you may be inspired to desire and work toward the love of God above all else in your life. You have a right, as you consider these teachings, to receive specific inspiration about how you can improve and strengthen your own life right now.

LOVE—WHAT IT IS

Godly love is powerfully defined in the Book of Mormon; it is one of the perfect attributes of Christ, called charity. "All men should have charity," Nephi said, "which charity is love. And except they should have charity they were nothing" (2 Nephi 26:30).

"Charity is the pure love of Christ . . . ; and whoso is found possessed of it at the last day, it shall be well with him" (Moroni 7:47).

"Charity suffereth long, and is kind, and envieth not [there is no resentment or discontent over the good fortune of others], and is not puffed up [there is no contention for superiority; those converted to Christ are not threatened by others' abilities and successes; there is no pride], seeketh not her own [there is no selfishness], is not easily provoked, thinketh no evil, and rejoiceth not in iniquity" (Moroni 7:45).

"I am filled with charity," exclaimed Moroni, "which is everlasting love" (Moroni 8:17).

LOVE—WHY WE WANT IT

We want the love of God because it is a commandment to love him and others. "Love the Lord thy God," the Lord commanded through Moses (Deuteronomy 6:5), and "love thy neighbour as thyself" (Leviticus 19:18). The grand secret is selflessness! The Lord revealed in modern times: "Thou shalt live together in love" (D&C 42:45), and "let thy love abound unto all men" (D&C 112:11). "Let thy bowels . . . be full of charity towards all men" (D&C 121:45).

Seeking and receiving the love of God is not just *a* commandment; it is *the* commandment, the number one of all commandments: "Above all these things put on charity" (Colossians 3:14); "above all things have fervent charity among yourselves: for charity shall cover the multitude of sins" (1 Peter 4:8); "above all things, clothe yourselves with the bond of charity" (D&C 88:125).

Getting the love of God in our hearts is a test: "The Lord your God proveth you, to know whether ye love the Lord your God with all your heart" (Deuteronomy 13:3). It is a proof of our discipleship: "By this shall all men know that ye are my disciples, if ye have love one to another" (John 13:35).

We want the love of God because it brings joy into our lives. "The love of God . . . is the most desirable above all things . . . and the most joyous to the soul" (1 Nephi 11:22–23). After the Savior's visit to the inhabitants of ancient America, Mormon was able to report that "there was no contention in the land, because of the love of God . . . in the hearts of the people [they did not have "a mind to injure one another"—see Mosiah 4:13] . . . ; and surely there could not be a happier people" (4 Nephi 1:15–16).

We want the love of God because we must have it to be able to successfully serve in his work and to get where we eventually want to be. "No one can assist in this work except he shall be humble and full of love" (D&C 12:8). "Wherefore, except men shall have charity they cannot inherit that place . . . prepared in the mansions of thy Father" (Ether 12:34).

LOVE—HOW WE GET IT

We can get God's love by being obedient to him. "If ye keep my commandments, ye shall abide in my love" (John 15:10). "Keep the commandments of God, that [you] might . . . be filled with love towards God and all men" (Mosiah 2:4).

We must also be willing to give up some things; in fact, we must be willing to sacrifice all things for the cause of Christ. Said he, "Greater love hath no man than this, that a man lay down his life for his friends" (John 15:13). Jesus offered this pointed challenge to the man he had set to lead the Church in the meridian of time: "Simon Peter, . . . lovest thou me more than these? . . . Feed my lambs. . . . Feed my sheep. . . . Feed my sheep" (John 21:15–17). We get God's love by dedicated service to others. "Teach them to love one another," King Benjamin declared, meaning that they must "serve one another" (Mosiah 4:15). "Succor those that stand in need" (Mosiah 4:16).

One specific thing we can do to have godly love in our lives is to keep ourselves clean, quickly expel immoral, lustful thoughts and feelings when they come, and maintain control of our physical desires. Alma counseled his son, "Bridle all your passions, that ye may be filled with love" (Alma 38:12).

Sincere prayer from our hearts is a key to obtaining the love of God. "Pray continually, that ye may . . . [be] full of love" (Alma 13:28). The prophet Mormon explained step by step how love comes: "Fulfilling the commandments bringeth remission of sins; and the remission of sins bringeth meekness, and lowliness of heart; and because of meekness and lowliness of heart cometh the visitation of the Holy Ghost, which Comforter filleth with hope and perfect love, which love endureth by diligence unto prayer" (Moroni 8:25–26). "Pray . . . with all the energy of heart, that ye may be filled with this love" (Moroni 7:48).

But doing all of the above is not sufficient. Love isn't something we can just work on, checking off each qualification on our checklist, then receive because we earned it. Instead, it is a gift. It is *the* gift of the Holy Ghost.

LOVE—STUMBLING BLOCKS TO WATCH OUT FOR

There are a few warnings in the scriptures about what to be careful of while working toward the gift of love. Along with his encouragement for us to pursue that greatest quality of godliness, Moroni advises: Do not "love money, and your substance, and your fine apparel . . . more than ye love the poor and the needy, the sick and the afflicted" (Mormon 8:37).

Paul cautions us not to let intellectual pursuits displace the quest for the infinitely more satisfying acquisition of love: "To know the love of Christ . . . passeth knowledge" (Ephesians 3:19); "knowledge puffeth up, but charity edifieth" (1 Corinthians 8:1); "though I . . . understand all mysteries, and all knowledge . . . , and have not charity, I am nothing" (1 Corinthians 13:2).

So we must be careful about money, worldly things, and intellectualism. They can distract us from the best possession of all.

LOVE—THE BLESSINGS OF HAVING IT

Paul learned by his own experience to prize the love of God that was granted to him, and he wrote in superlative terms about the mighty changes that can come to those who likewise experience this greatest gift: "Eye hath not seen, nor ear heard, neither have entered into the heart of man, the things which God hath prepared for them that love him" (1 Corinthians 2:9). "All things work together for good to them that love God" (Romans 8:28).

John, the same that we call "the Beloved" because of his possessing the gift of love, wrote: "Every one that loveth is born of God, and knoweth God . . . ; for God is love" (1 John 4:7–8). John also knew the serenity that can come into the life of one who is filled with the love of Christ, for "love casteth out fear" (1 John 4:18).

One of our elders was concerned about returning home to an inactive family after his mission, but he wrote just before leaving for home: "There is no fear in love. I learned that while studying my scriptures, while trying to answer the question: 'How can I call my mother and my family to the tree of life?' (1 Nephi 8:15)—the answer came to my mind so clearly: 'With love; just as you've always done.' I felt that perfect love, and from that time I've not had any fear of returning home, nor will I have."

Moroni described how we can achieve the ultimate reward of becoming like God and dwelling with him: "Deny yourselves of all ungodliness, and love God with all your might, mind and strength, then . . . by his grace ye may be perfect in Christ" (Moroni 10:32).

Spiritual preparedness, the readiness to dwell in God's presence, which involves "sanctification through the grace of our Lord . . . , [is given] to all those who love and serve God" (D&C 20:31).

LOVE—ITS INFLUENCE IN YOUR PERSONAL LIFE

To have the pure love of Christ means that you are praying fervently every day. You are studying the scriptures and writing new impressions, the revelation that comes while you are in the Spirit. You are testifying of the Savior and of his work to everyone that you can. You are learning to love every person who comes into your life.

When you have the pure love of Christ, you do more than just try to "get along" with others. There is a reason I don't like the phrase "getting along." In early 1967 I used that phrase in one of my weekly reports from Paraná, Argentina, to my mission president, Richard G. Scott. I wrote that "my companion and I are getting along OK; we have some minor companionship problems as I suppose all missionaries do."

Well, that was the subject of our next zone conference. President Scott quoted from my report (without mentioning my name) and taught us that good, successful missionaries don't just "get along"—they learn to love each other.

When you love God, you keep his commandments; you are obedient and happy. You are constant, or, as the Book of Mormon says, "firm and steadfast" (see 1 Nephi 2:10; Helaman 15:8; 3 Nephi 6:14). You can be trusted. You do things for the right reasons. There are three degrees of glory in our obedience: telestial is obedience out of obligation, but begrudgingly; terrestrial is obedience out of duty, but willingly; celestial is obedience out of love of God and man. You delight in obeying all truth that you know because you love God, the father of all truth.

Having examined many great teachings of the Savior and the prophets about love, there is perhaps one more element that should be emphasized. It comes out of an experience I had near the end of our mission in Chile. One of the missionaries who was about to depart for home stood to bear his final testimony. He testified, "I learned to love here in Chile. I love the people. I love God." Then he went on to explain that in the previous few weeks he had talked with all those he had baptized (even though going back or telephoning back to former areas of service was against the rules), and he had given little kisses and hugs to the grandmas (also against the rules). Interesting, I thought, how people rationalize and justify their behavior. He testified that he had learned to love—but he didn't learn obedience. Jesus said, "If ye love me, keep my commandments." It is true that love is the highest quality of godliness, but *it is not all.*

The elder I admired most during my mission in Argentina decades ago, my ideal, my model among missionaries, knew how to love people into the Church. He was incredibly successful in bringing people to the waters of baptism. But years after the mission he was excommunicated from the Church for disobedience to the laws of the land and the laws of God. Love and obedience are an indispensable combination.

THE KEY IS LOVE

In recent years a number of books have been published about near-death experiences—what individuals have learned from brief encounters with loved ones in the world of spirits. Without necessarily endorsing the following people's experiences, I find a most important truth represented in them. Our highest objective is to bring people to Christ—and to bring them to the love of Christ. Moroni said that in the end, if we have charity it will be well with us. The first and great commandment is to love the Lord. The next most important is to love our neighbor (see Moroni 7:47; Mark 12:30–31).

How insignificant will be the money we have made, the things we have accumulated, or the fun we have had—if we don't have love. This is one of the messages we glean from the following near-death experiences.

From George G. Ritchie, M.D.:

"How we spend our time on earth, the kind of relationships we build, is vastly, infinitely more important than we can know."[2]

Describing the Being of light, Dr. Ritchie wrote: "I knew that this Man loved me. Far more even than power, what emanated from this Presence was . . . an astonishing love. A love beyond my wildest imagining."[3]

"The question, like everything else proceeding from Him, had to do with love. How much have you loved with your life? Have you loved others as I am loving you?"[4]

"If I wanted to feel the nearness of Christ—and I did want that, above everything else—I would have to find it in the people that He put before me each day."[5]

From Raymond A. Moody Jr., M.D.:

Reviewing commonalities or parallels in people's near-death

experiences, Dr. Moody wrote: "The being seems to stress the importance of two things in life: Learning to love other people and acquiring knowledge."[6]

"Almost everyone [with a near-death experience] has stressed the importance in this life of trying to cultivate love for others, a love of a unique and profound kind."[7]

From RaNelle Wallace:

Describing part of her experience in the world of spirits: "I saw a scene that changed me forever. The scene was sacred beyond words, beyond expression, and those who have witnessed it keep it hidden in their hearts. I saw that I had indeed lacked faith, that love isn't simply a word or an emotion; love is a power that gives action to all around it. *Love is the power of life.* This was a turning point for me, something that allowed all of my understanding and love to magnify, but I can never share the details here except to say that I know that love between people here can be eternal."[8]

Just before RaNelle Wallace's spirit returned to her physical body, her grandmother in the spirit world said to her: "'There is one more thing I need to say to you. Tell everybody that the key is love. The key is love,' she repeated. 'The key is love,' she said a third time."[9]

9

IT'S YOUR CHOICE

YOU CAN GET YOUR SINS BLOTTED OUT, or your name will be blotted out. You can be sealed to God or sealed to the devil. You can remain an enemy to God or become a friend of God. You can decide on eternal life or eternal death. It's your choice.

One of the crucial decisions in the lives of two contemporaries, Lot and Melchizedek, was their selection of where to live. Lot "pitched his tent toward Sodom" (Genesis 13:12), and later "dwelt in Sodom" (Genesis 14:12). That decision cost him his family. Lot apparently had made the decision based on the attractive nature of the properties down in the Jordan Valley—"It was well watered every where, . . . even as the garden of the Lord" (Genesis 13:10)—even though the low morals of the people should have been a warning sign.

Melchizedek, on the other hand, lived with his people in the top of the hill country in a city called Peace (Salem).

It is quite a contrast. Lot chose to live at the bottom of the world (the Jordan Rift Valley around the Dead Sea is literally the lowest spot on earth), while Melchizedek chose to live up in the highest part of the land with his people—who eventually became righteous enough to be translated from the earth (see JST Genesis 14:34). Lot, along with his wife and children, were subjected to the lowest kind of life in Sodom, while Melchizedek, along with his wife and children as we suppose, lived on "higher ground" and enjoyed the blessings of being closer to God, physically and spiritually, likely enjoying the highest blessings available to God's children on earth in the holy sanctuary, or temple, in Salem.[1]

The lesson seems clear: Choose the higher ground to avoid evil. Don't even pitch your tent *toward* Sodom—don't even approach the evil. Lot's daughters committed gross immorality (see Genesis 19:30–36). And where did they learn that kind of behavior? Perhaps when their father pitched his tent toward Sodom.

Are you pitching your tent toward Sodom or toward Salem? The king of Sodom was the king of wickedness; the king of Salem was the king of righteousness (the literal meaning of the name Melchizedek).

You choose to follow either wickedness or righteousness. If you expose yourself to immorality very long, it dulls your abhorrence of sin. At first you are shocked, then you tolerate it, then you experiment with it, then you embrace it. On the other hand, if you constantly expose yourself to moral purity, fortified by daily diligence in prayer and scripture study, and by regular service to others and regular temple worship, you will build up a spiritual defense system to repulse the fiery darts of the adversary (the gross, crass, and vulgar things of the world) and be attracted only to that which is uplifting, edifying, and sanctifying. It's your choice. You choose to live the low life, without standards, or the godly life, with high standards. You choose to embrace the darkness or embrace the light.

As noted above, you are choosing by your daily behavior whether you get your sins blotted out (see Isaiah 43:25; Acts 3:19) or your name blotted out (see Mosiah 26:36; Moroni 6:7; D&C 20:83). You will be either sealed to God (see Mosiah 5:15) or sealed to the devil (see Alma 34:35). You will remain an enemy to God, the natural man (see Mosiah 3:19), or you will become a friend of God, as was Abraham (see

Isaiah 41:8; James 2:23). Our Father and our Savior invite us to put off the natural man and become their friends (see D&C 84:77; 98:1). God, in his righteous anger, will either visit upon you the evil of your doings (see Jeremiah 23:2; Alma 9:12), or he will visit you in mercy and with his Spirit and in the joy of his countenance (see 2 Nephi 4:26; Alma 17:10; D&C 88:53).

The scriptures are full of choices. You can either labor in sin (see Jacob 2:5) or labor in love (see Hebrews 6:10). You will either want to cover yourself and hide your sins (see Proverbs 28:13; Alma 12:14; D&C 121:37), or the Lord will cover your sins for you. The meaning of the Hebrew term for atonement (*kippur*) is "covering up." The Savior literally covers up our sins and remembers them no more (see Psalms 32:1; 85:2; Romans 4:7; D&C 58:42). You can cast off your sins (see Alma 13:27), or you will be cast off (see 1 Nephi 10:21; Alma 22:6; Helaman 12:25).

Everyone likes gifts. According to the word of the Lord, you may choose to receive good gifts of God and the Spirit, or evil gifts, attractively packaged and presented by the devil and his followers (see Moroni 10:30; D&C 46:8–26). You choose a well of water springing up into everlasting life (see John 4:14; D&C 63:23) or a fountain of filthy water (see

1 Nephi 12:16). It's your choice of eternal life or eternal death (see 2 Nephi 10:23). You can have your destruction made sure (see Helaman 13:32, 38) or your salvation made sure (see 2 Peter 1:10; D&C 131:5).

If you are not caught up in the deceptions of the world, you may be caught up to come with the Lord in glory (see Joseph Smith—Matthew 1:44–45; D&C 88:96). In the end the devil will not support you (see Alma 30:60), but God will support you (see Alma 44:4). You can become a child of the devil (see Alma 5:41) or a child of God (see Moroni 7:48; D&C 34:3; Moses 6:68).

As missionaries trying to teach a man in Argentina decades ago, my companion and I taught the discussion presenting the plan of salvation, including the options for our future life, when the man abruptly cut us off by saying, "Don't talk to me about any more life. I hate *this* life. I don't want any *more* life!" Needless to say that shook us up a little. We didn't really know how to continue. According to our Latter-day Saint philosophy, the purpose of life is more life. As I have thought about that learning experience over the years, I have arrived at some conclusions. Actually, we don't have a choice about whether we will live forever or not. It is a fact. All of us are going to become immortal and live forever (see 1 Corinthians 15:22; Alma 11:42–44). The choice we do have is where we are going to live, in what condition we are going to live, and with whom we are going to live. You are deciding your destiny by how you live every day.

It's your choice. You can spend numerous hours on the Internet, including a menu of sleazy, pornographic sites, or you can spend those same hours reading the scriptures, Church magazines, biographies of Church presidents, and other such literature—the kind that invariably inspires and edifies.

You can frequently indulge in overeating and gluttonous stuffing with unhealthy fast foods, or you can show self-restraint by eating a moderate, healthy diet and observing a monthly fast, even fasting on other occasions as the need arises.

You can constantly work and spend money in order to buy all the luxuries and comforts of this world; or you can work hard to provide adequately for your family, sacrifice through paying tithes and offerings or serving missions, and build the kingdom of God on the earth.

You can be a fan of Hollywood and go to see all the new movies as they are released, and follow the popular weekly shows on television, or you can follow the counsel of Church leaders and avoid movies and TV programs that contain violence, profanity, sexual insinuations, and immodesty.

You can make Sunday a day of yard work, travel, and entertainment, or you can follow the prophets' counsel to keep the Sabbath holy by attending all Church meetings and avoiding shopping, eating at restaurants, attending or participating in sporting events, and other worldly activities.

You can express dissatisfaction, frustration, annoyance, and anger by pridefully criticizing family members, Church leaders, and others, or you can repent daily of improper and unkind feelings such as anger, impatience, sarcasm, and cynicism, knowing that anger and irritation are wrong—even if you are in the right.

You can fill your evenings and weekends with thrill-producing activities and entertainment, thus crowding out any spiritually energizing opportunities, or you can discover that frequent, alert temple attendance is a major source of power and strength in your life.

THE PRINCIPLE OF CHOICE IN THE SCRIPTURES

The Lord has been unequivocal in his instructions about our rights and our duties with regard to agency. He said to the first man, Adam: "Thou mayest choose for thyself, for it is given unto thee" (Moses 3:17). Joshua admonished his people: "Choose you this day whom ye will serve" (Joshua 24:15). And Elijah counseled his people: "How long halt ye between two opinions? if the Lord be God, follow him: but if Baal, then follow him" (1 Kings 18:21).

Lehi taught his son Jacob that "the Lord God gave unto man that he should act for himself. Wherefore, man could not act for himself save it should be that he was enticed by the one or the other. . . . Men are free . . . to choose liberty and eternal life . . . or to choose captivity and death" (2 Nephi 2:16, 27). Jacob taught: "Ye are free to act for yourselves—to choose the way of everlasting death or the way of eternal life" (2 Nephi 10:23).

Samuel, the Lamanite prophet, gave this splendid two-verse sermon on agency: "Ye are free; ye are permitted to act for yourselves; for behold, God hath given unto you a knowledge and he hath made you free. He hath given unto you that ye might know good from evil, and he hath given unto you that ye might choose life or death; and ye can do good and . . . have that which is good restored unto you; or ye can do evil, and have that which is evil restored unto you" (Helaman 14:30–31).

Elder Bruce R. McConkie observed that for a Latter-day

Saint, agency means to do it willingly or to do it anyway![2] The Lord has explained that he does not permit any real Latter-day Saint to live in conformity with the ways of the world (see D&C 95:13). He has called us out of the world; we are to live in the world, but not live a worldly life. He has high expectations that we will, through our own experience, learn to use our freedom of choice to support and promote righteousness. We cannot walk with one foot in the kingdom and the other foot in the world. In the last days we cannot "halt between two opinions."

In a sense, you must take sides. You are either on the Lord's side or you are on the devil's side. You either adopt the lifestyle of the Savior and become one with him or you adopt the lifestyle of the devil and become one with him. You either yield to the enticings of Satan (see Helaman 6:26; Moroni 7:12), or you yield to the enticings of the Holy Ghost (see Mosiah 3:19; Moroni 7:13). There are varied voices whispering for your attention and allegiance. You choose which voice you will listen to.

Elder Boyd K. Packer explained: "In the Church we are not neutral. We are one-sided. There is a war going on, and we are engaged in it. It is the war between good and evil, and we are belligerents defending the good. We are therefore obliged to give preference to and protect all that is represented in the gospel of Jesus Christ, and we have made covenants to do it."[3]

SATAN'S CHEAP IMITATIONS OF DIVINE TRUTHS

As you consider your choices, you need to watch out for counterfeits. Satan has always sponsored imitations or cheap counterparts to God's sacred principles and practices. For example, temples are the holiest structures on earth, where the most important ordinances required for exaltation are received. The devil's counterparts, pagan temples, have been part of all the ancient cultures. Sumerians, Egyptians, Assyrians, Babylonians, Canaanites, Persians, Greeks, Romans, and many others had their sanctuaries where ceremonies and practices, even such gross perversions as cultic prostitution, were carried out.

Priesthood is the power of God used to perform holy ordinances and bless the lives of people. Satan came along early in our world's history with priestcraft, his alternative distortion of true priesthood. Priestcrafts involve attempting to bless one's own life, and building up and glorifying one's self, instead of blessing the people.

An oath is a promise or commitment, or to use a more

sacred word, it is a covenant. You can either make an oath with God, openly affirming the oath by the word of truth and integrity, or you can make an oath with the devil, secretly affirming the oath by the word of falsehood and deceit.

One of the most sacred privileges in mortality is for humans to participate with God in the creation of new life, to procreate and help the God of heaven continue his work and his glory in providing opportunity for mortal life and eternal life for his children. That sacred privilege involves the physical union of a man and a woman. The sacred uniting of a man and a woman in sexual relations is one of the beautiful and elevating experiences our Father has provided for his children on this earth. Of course, Satan would attempt to strike at that sacred power right from the beginning, encouraging humans to abuse those powers of procreation, getting them to indulge their physical desires whenever and with whomever they want. Go ahead and prostitute those godly powers, the devil whispers, and call it "love." His depraved counterfeits are not love, of course, but lust.

FORWARD AND UPWARD

If you want to be secretive and hide what you are listening to in your CD or DVD player or what you are calling up on the computer or what rental movie you are bringing into your home; if you want to keep parents and leaders in the dark about some illegal substance you are using or some illicit relationship you are having with another person—if you are doing these things, then you are operating in the realm of darkness, where you would prefer that Christ not shed any of his light on you. But in the end there will be nothing hidden, nothing that will not be brought to light (see Luke 8:17; 2 Nephi 30:17; Mormon 5:8; D&C 1:2–3).

We all choose whether we will live in heaven or hell. The Savior has paid for and resolved every consequence of the Fall: the first transgression, the demands of the law of justice, the physical death, and the spiritual death.

We cannot properly blame any ancestor, or even our parents, for our own misbehavior. We have the ability and freedom to choose. We cannot complain about the demands of justice, because the Lord has provided the perfect balance and solution: his mercy and grace.

We cannot legitimately decry the effects of physical and spiritual death, because our Redeemer has totally overcome the effects of physical death by giving each and every one a guarantee of resurrection to immortality, and he has provided for our return to the Father's presence (see 2 Nephi 2:10; 9:22,

38; Alma 11:41, 44; 42:23; Helaman 14:15–17; Mormon 9:12–14).

Once we have been escorted back into God's presence, whether we can stay there or not is up to each one of us. We are deciding by our daily behavior whether or not we will endure his light and goodness and continue to dwell with him forever.

Like Lot and Melchizedek, we decide where we will live and how we will live. It really is our choice; and it has eternal implications. Mighty changes can go either direction. For a Latter-day Saint the only real choice is forward and upward.

HEAVEN STARTS HERE

The Father and the Savior are not neutral, sitting as arbitrary judges, waiting to see the outcome of our choices. They are working hard to promote our eternal welfare. They've spent an unfathomable amount of energy and effort in creating worlds, or "school grounds," for their children to learn the lessons of godliness. They have done and are continuing to do all they can to secure our exaltation.

They are on our side, extending every mercy and every heavenly favor to see that we return Home. They yearn to share everything they have with us. They want all the best for us, because they love us. Their reaching out to us is infinite. If we're working hard to be on their side, their loving kindness knows no bounds.

Before you get to heaven it's important to stop and realize that you're already experiencing traces of heaven here and now. You don't have to wait for the ultimate eternal package of blessings in distant time and space; you can be partaking of heavenly joys right now.

If you are exercising mighty faith, repenting, praying, treasuring up God's words, keeping the Spirit, being exactly obedient, getting rid of pride, and cultivating the love of God, you are already enjoying the blessings of heaven.

Later comes the *fulness* of such blessings, but you can taste them here. You are already getting well acquainted with your Father in Heaven; you're spending countless mortal hours talking with him. You are getting well acquainted with your Savior by spending numerous hours pondering his words and works—and in the process you're becoming like him. Heaven starts here.

Appendix 1

WHAT THE LORD SAYS ABOUT PRAYER

INSTRUCTIONS: READ AND PONDER THE following ten sections, writing a sentence about the essential message of each scripture passage; then write a page describing your feelings, goals, and testimony about prayer. Follow up with determined effort to live your goals.

WHY PRAY?

Alma 5:45–47
Alma 7:23
3 Nephi 18:15, 18–19
Moroni 7:48; 8:26
D&C 31:12

HOW TO PRAY?

3 Nephi 18:21
3 Nephi 19:6
D&C 9:7–9
D&C 19:28
D&C 23:6

IN WHAT SPIRIT?

Matthew 6:5–8
Mark 11:24–26
James 1:5–8
1 Nephi 15:7–11
Mosiah 4:11
Alma 38:13–14
3 Nephi 19:24, 32–33
Moroni 7:6–9, 48

PRAY FOR WHAT?

2 Nephi 32:8–9
Mosiah 27:14
Alma 13:27–29
Alma 34:18–27
3 Nephi 12:44
Moroni 10:4
D&C 50:29
Joseph Smith—History 1:29

WHERE TO PRAY?

Alma 34:21, 26

WHEN TO PRAY?

Daniel 6:10
1 Thessalonians 5:17
Mosiah 4:11
Alma 34:21
Alma 37:37

ANY WARNINGS OR LIMITATIONS?

James 4:3
2 Nephi 4:35
Alma 38:13
Helaman 10:4–5
Ether 2:14–15
D&C 88:64–65

WITH WHAT PROMISE?

Matthew 7:7–11
Matthew 21:22
1 Nephi 18:3
Mosiah 4:11–16
D&C 6:11

D&C 10:5
D&C 19:38
D&C 42:14
D&C 112:10

2 Nephi 33:3
Enos 1:1–12
Alma 8:10

THEN WHAT?

Omni 1:26
Alma 7:22–24
Alma 34:28

EXAMPLES OF "PLEADING"

Isaiah 38:1–5
2 Nephi 4:15–35

MEDITATE ON THESE WORDS

"*Pleading*"

"*He prayed more earnestly*" (referring to the Savior in Gethsemane)—Luke 22:44

"*Mighty prayer*"—Enos 1:4; D&C 5:24

Appendix 2

WHAT THE LORD SAYS ABOUT REPENTANCE

INSTRUCTIONS: FOR REAL SPIRITUAL BENEFIT, take the necessary time to study and ponder the following scripture passages, giving each of them serious thought. Write a sentence or two about the essential meaning of each passage, and personalize your sentences using first-person pronouns ("I should . . ."). When finished with all sections, write about your feelings, goals, and testimony of repentance; then prayerfully identify something you need to repent of, and put all this into practice.

THE COMMANDMENT

Acts 17:30
2 Nephi 9:23

2 Nephi 26:27
Alma 5:32–33
3 Nephi 11:32
3 Nephi 27:20
D&C 6:9

PURPOSES OF REPENTANCE

Mark 1:4
Alma 12:24
Moroni 8:25
D&C 49:13

GODLY SORROW AND SUFFERING NECESSARY

Psalm 38:17–18
Ezekiel 16:61 (first two lines)
2 Corinthians 7:10
Mosiah 27:28–29
Alma 42:29
D&C 1:27

CONFESSION NECESSARY

Ezra 10:11
Mosiah 26:29
D&C 58:43

RESTITUTION NECESSARY

Leviticus 6:4
Numbers 5:7
Ezekiel 33:15–16
Mosiah 27:35

FORSAKING NECESSARY

Proverbs 28:13
Isaiah 1:16
Ezekiel 18:21
Mosiah 4:10
D&C 58:43

AFTER REPENTANCE, GOOD WORKS NECESSARY

Acts 26:20
Alma 5:54
Helaman 12:23–24
D&C 1:32
D&C 18:41–43

OUR OBLIGATION TO FORGIVE OTHERS

Luke 17:3–4
Mosiah 26:31
D&C 64:8–10

CONSEQUENCES OF NOT REPENTING

Luke 13:3
Jacob 3:3 (first half)
Mosiah 2:38
Alma 5:31, 51
Alma 34:33–35
3 Nephi 9:2
D&C 1:33
D&C 5:19
D&C 19:4
D&C 42:28

REWARDS OF REPENTING

Mosiah 4:3
Mosiah 27:24–29

Alma 7:14–16
Alma 26:22
Alma 32:13
Helaman 5:11, 41
3 Nephi 9:22
3 Nephi 27:16
D&C 15:6
D&C 18:13–16
D&C 58:42 (and Isaiah 38:17)

EXAMPLES OF REPENTANCE

Read slowly and ponder the message of the following great illustrations of how repentance works.

Enos 1:2–8
Alma 22:15–18
Alma 36:12–21

Appendix 3

WHAT THE LORD SAYS ABOUT HOW TO GET THE SPIRIT

2 Nephi 4:15–16
Mosiah 3:19
Mosiah 4:11
Mosiah 5:7
Mosiah 18:10
Alma 5:14–15
Alma 5:45–46
3 Nephi 12:6
3 Nephi 18:7
D&C 88:67
D&C 121:45–46

NOTES

CHAPTER 1: HOW TO HAVE MIGHTY SCRIPTURE STUDY

1. From a conversation of the author with Joseph Fielding McConkie, February 18, 2004.
2. Boyd K. Packer, "The Mystery of Life," *Ensign,* November 1983, 17.
3. *Doctrines of the Restoration: Sermons and Writings of Bruce R. McConkie,* edited and arranged by Mark L. McConkie (Salt Lake City: Bookcraft, 1989), 238.
4. Joseph Smith, *History of The Church of Jesus Christ of Latter-day Saints,* edited by B. H. Roberts, 7 vols., 2d ed. rev. (Salt Lake City: The Church of Jesus Christ of Latter-day Saints, 1932–51), 2:199.
5. Boyd K. Packer, Conference Report, October 1986, 20.
6. Harold B. Lee, "Using the Scriptures in Our Church Assignments," *Improvement Era,* January 1969, 13.

CHAPTER 2: HOW TO HAVE MIGHTY PRAYER

1. *Noah Webster's First Edition of an American Dictionary of the English Language* (San Francisco: Foundation for American Christian Education), s.v. "importune."

CHAPTER 3: HOW TO HAVE MIGHTY FAITH

1. See Jeffrey R. Holland, *However Long and Hard the Road* (Salt Lake City: Deseret Book, 1985), 33; and Robert D. Hales, Conference Report, October 1981, 26.

Notes

2. Joseph Smith, *Lectures on Faith* (Salt Lake City: Deseret Book, 1985), 6:7.
3. Heber J. Grant "Dream, O Youth!" *Improvement Era,* September 1941, 524.
4. Gordon B. Hinckley, "Don't Be a Pickle Sucker," BYU devotional speech, 1974.
5. Quoted by Jack H. Goaslind, "Look to the Future with Optimism," *Ensign,* April 1997, 25.
6. Robert Frost, *A Masque of Reason* (New York: Henry Holt and Co., 1945).

Chapter 4: How to Enjoy Mighty Repentance

1. Ezra Taft Benson, *God, Family, Country: Our Three Great Loyalties* (Salt Lake City: Deseret Book, 1974), 196.
2. Spencer W. Kimball, "Love versus Lust," Brigham Young University *Speeches of the Year,* Provo, Utah, 5 January 1965, 10.
3. Richard G. Scott, Conference Report, October 1994, 52.
4. *The Teachings of Ezra Taft Benson* (Salt Lake City: Bookcraft, 1988), 285.
5. Truman G. Madsen, "The Commanding Image of Christ," Brigham Young University *Speeches of the Year,* Provo, Utah, 16 November 1965, 8.
6. Ezra Taft Benson, "A Mighty Change of Heart," *Ensign,* October 1989, 5.
7. Dallin H. Oaks, *The Lord's Way* (Salt Lake City: Deseret Book, 1991), 225–26.

Chapter 5: How to Get and Keep the Spirit

1. Brigham Young, in *Journal of Discourses,* 26 vols. (Liverpool: F. D. and S. W. Richards, 1855–86), 9:141; emphasis added.
2. *Teachings of the Prophet Joseph Smith,* selected and arranged by Joseph Fielding Smith (Salt Lake City: Deseret Book, 1976), 328.
3. Heber C. Kimball, in *Journal of Discourses,* 4:222.
4. *The Teachings of Howard W. Hunter,* edited by Clyde J. Williams (Salt Lake City: Bookcraft, 1997), 184–85.

Chapter 6: How to Be Exactly Obedient

1. *Hymns of The Church of Jesus Christ of Latter-day Saints* (Salt Lake City: The Church of Jesus Christ of Latter-day Saints, 1985), no. 195.
2. Bruce R. McConkie, *Mormon Doctrine,* 2d ed. rev. (Salt Lake City:

176

Bookcraft, 1966), 539; see also Joseph F. Smith, in *Journal of Discourses,* 26 vols. (Liverpool: F. D. and S. W. Richards, 1855–86), 16:248.

3. Spencer W. Kimball, Conference Report, October 1954, 54.
4. Ibid., 51–52.
5. Bruce R. McConkie, in *Studies in Scripture, Volume Three: The Old Testament,* edited by Kent P. Jackson and Robert L. Millet (Salt Lake City: Randall Book Company, 1985), 57.
6. *Teachings of the Prophet Joseph Smith,* selected and arranged by Joseph Fielding Smith (Salt Lake City: Deseret Book, 1976), 256.
7. Brigham Young, in *Journal of Discourses,* 7:55.
8. Eliza R. Snow, "How Great the Widsom and the Love," *Hymns,* no. 195.

CHAPTER 7: HOW TO GET RID OF PRIDE

1. C. S. Lewis, *Mere Christianity* (San Francisco: HarperSanFrancisco, 1952, 1980), 121–23.
2. *Teachings of the Prophet Joseph Smith,* selected and arranged by Joseph Fielding Smith (Salt Lake City: Deseret Book, 1976), 155.
3. Ibid., 258–59.
4. Ibid., 241.
5. *The Discourses of Wilford Woodruff,* selected, arranged, and edited by G. Homer Durham (Salt Lake City: Bookcraft, 1969), 123–24.
6. Ezra Taft Benson, "Beware of Pride," *Ensign,* May 1989, 4–7.

CHAPTER 8: HOW TO OBTAIN THE LOVE OF CHRIST

1. Quoted in author's personal journal, 15 February 1999.
2. George G. Ritchie, *Return from Tomorrow* (Old Tappan, New Jersey: Fleming H. Revell Company, 1978), 16.
3. Ibid., 49.
4. Ibid., 54.
5. Ibid., 111.
6. Raymond A. Moody Jr., *Life After Life* (New York: Bantam Books, 1975), 65.
7. Ibid., 92.
8. RaNelle Wallace, *The Burning Within* (Carson City, Nevada: Gold Leaf Press, 1994), 105.
9. Ibid., 116.

Notes

CHAPTER 9: IT'S YOUR CHOICE

1. See David B. Galbraith, D. Kelly Ogden, and Andrew C. Skinner, *Jerusalem, The Eternal City* (Salt Lake City: Deseret Book, 1996), 30–31, 36.
2. Conversation of the author with Joseph Fielding McConkie, February 18, 2004.
3. Boyd K. Packer, "The Mantle Is Far, Far Greater Than the Intellect," in *Charge to Religious Educators,* 2nd ed. (Salt Lake City: The Church of Jesus Christ of Latter-day Saints, 1982), 35.

INDEX

Index

Index

observing grandson walking, 33;
key questions to ask, 33
Pride: experience watching movie,
119; definition of broken heart,
119–20; C. S. Lewis on,
120–23; as a particularly
harmful sin, 123; overcoming
the natural man, 123–24; and
gaining strength and
nourishment from the true
Vine, 124–26; experience at
petting farm, 125; having a
willingness to be dependent,
125–27; Joseph Smith on, 128;
Ezra Taft Benson on, 133–37
Pride, resisting the spirit of: taking
responsibility for your own
problems, 128–29; avoiding
contention and criticism,
129–31; Joseph Smith, 131;
realizing you are not
indispensable, 132–33; Wilford
Woodruff on feeling you are
indispensable, 132–33

Remembering the Savior, as a
prerequisite to obtaining the
Spirit, 94
Repentance, mighty: importance
of, 52–53; Greek and Hebrew
words for, 53; definition of,
53–54; Ezra Taft Benson on
sorrow for sin, 55; experience
with cancer on nose, 55–56;
necessity of godly sorrow and
suffering, 55–59; "Four Faces of
Repentance" illustration, 56–58;

Spencer W. Kimball on
confession, 59; necessity of
confession, 59–60; Richard G.
Scott on premeditated sin, 60;
death of daughter's friend,
60–61; importance of not
procrastinating, 60–62; death of
returned missionary, 61; Ezra
Taft Benson on avoiding sin, 62;
necessity of restitution, 62–63;
definition of forsaking sin, 63;
experiences with missionaries at
MTC, 63–64, 66; necessity of
forsaking sin, 63–67; forgetting
your sins, 64–66, 72–73;
becoming a new person, 66–67;
experience losing document on
computer, 67–68; necessity of
good works after, 67–70;
experience of converted student,
69–70; importance of forgiving
others, 70–71; consequences of
not repenting, 71–72; knowing
when you have been forgiven,
72–73; rewards for, 72–77;
understanding the depths of
Christ's forgiveness, 74–75;
experience making erasures on
student papers, 75–76; Ezra Taft
Benson on, 76–77; experience
with advertisement offering
cleansing products, 77–78;
baptism and, 79–80; partaking
of the sacrament and, 80;
Dallin H. Oaks on the power of,
80–81; ability of Christ to repair
the damage of sin, 81–82;

Index